ENCOUNTERING GOD

Encountering God

Joyce Huggett

Hodder & Stoughton
LONDON SYDNEY AUCKLAND

First published in Great Britain 1995

The right of Joyce Huggett to be identified as the Author of
this Work has been asserted by her in accordance with the
Copyright, Designs and Patents Act 1988.

10 9 8 7 6 5 4 3 2 1

British Library Cataloguing in Publication Data
A record for this book is available from the British Library

ISBN 0 340 64263 7

Bible references are from the New International Version unless
otherwise stated.

Typeset by Hewer Text Composition Services, Edinburgh
Printed and bound in Great Britain by
Cox & Wyman Ltd., Reading, Berkshire

Hodder and Stoughton
A division of Hodder Headline PLC
338 Euston Road
London NW1 3BH

For Lisa
with gratitude to God
for our friendship

Contents

Introduction

They heard the sound of the Lord God moving about in the garden in the cool of the day. (Genesis 3:8)

God is always coming, and we, like Adam, hear his footsteps.
God is always coming because He is life,
  and life has the unbridled force of creation.
God comes because He is light,
  and light may not remain hidden.
God comes because He is love,
  and love needs to give of itself.
God has always been coming; God is always coming.[1]

So claimed Carlo Carretto, who goes on to ask: 'How does He come? Does He come as a cloud or as a person? Does He come as a person, or does He come through His words, spoken two thousand years ago and transmitted by the Evangelists in the gospels?'[2]

My aim in producing this month-long set of reflections is to help readers to discover for themselves how God has been coming to them in the past, how he comes to them today, and how he might come to them in the future.

As the overall title of this series of small books implies, we are envisaging that readers will spend some twenty minutes per day ruminating on one portion of the book. I would like to suggest that a generous slice of that twenty-minute time slot should be given to responding to God's invitation through the Psalmist, 'Be still and know that I am God' (Psalm 46:10). By stillness, I mean handing over the pressures, the pain and the pleasures of the moment to God, tuning in to his presence and his love, nestling at his feet, as it were, so that our focus changes from self to him. The reason for this suggestion is that, when we still ourselves in this way, we view life, our life, from a renewed perspective – not ours but God's. In that still place we are also far more likely to discern precisely how he wants to come to us at this particular moment in time.

Having spent at least five minutes relaxing, unwinding and becoming aware of God's presence, we will be in a better position to absorb his Word. I suggest that we read the verses quoted as slowly as possible, letting their nurturing or challenging truths trickle from our heads into our hearts.

After the Bible quotation comes an excerpt from one of my books testifying, usually from personal experience, to the way in which these particular verses still have meaning today. These excerpts are intended to spark off thoughts and memories in you, the reader.

Carlo Carretto suggests, and I agree with him, that 'God's presence is obvious to anyone who can hear His footsteps.' The aim of the section entitled 'Reflection' is to help you to detect his footsteps – past, present and future.

When God revealed himself to the Apostle John on the island of Patmos, he gave him these instructions: 'Write on a scroll what you see . . .' (Revelation 1:11). Years before, he had given the prophet Habbakuk a similar task: 'Write down the revelation' (Habakkuk 2:2). For centuries, Christians have discovered the value of recording in some way what God shows them, and their response to his revelation and his many comings. That is why, each day, spaces have been left for you to make journal-type jottings if you would like to. Sometimes these may be verbal, sometimes pictorial, and sometimes diagrammatic.

This series is designed, not just for individuals, but for prayer triplets, prayer groups, home fellowships, couples or for friends who meet to pray together. When using the book with others, in addition to responding to the reflections in writing or with a drawing, there would be value in sharing some of the thoughts, reactions and feelings which have been prompted by the meditation.

But perhaps this series of booklets should carry a warning. The more we hear God and the more we encounter him, the deeper our longing for him will become. Soon we shall grow dissatisfied with a twenty-minute-per-day prayer time. We shall find ourselves longing to spend more time with this God who comes. That is not impossible. For most of us, on our day off, for example, we can schedule into our organisers or diaries a whole hour simply 'to be' with God. Once a month we may be able to plot into our busy lives an entire morning, an evening or even a Quiet Day, just to be in the presence of the God who comes. We can do this on our own or with others. And once a year, perhaps, we can begin to think in terms of going away on retreat where we can be really still – to let God set the agenda, to rest with him, to respond to Jesus's invitation: 'Come apart with me . . . and rest' (Mark 6:31).

Meanwhile I pray that, when you use this book and as a result of reflecting in the ways I suggest, you will find yourself praying the prayer the Bride of Christ prays with such longing and yearning:

'Come, Lord Jesus.' (Revelation 22:20)

1

Through the memory

Reading: Deuteronomy 8:2

Remember how the Lord your God led you all the way in the desert these forty years, to humble you and to test you in order to know what was in your heart.

Our memory is a God-given gift. God uses it to show us how near he has been to us in the moments when we have not been aware of him. He uses it, too, to persuade us that, even though we have not been conscious of his activity, he has been and is at work in us. That is why, almost every day, I set aside five minutes when I tune in to God's presence and, with God, I watch an action replay of the previous twenty-four hours. In this time, I bring into sharp focus only those moments which have been pleasurable for some reason. When I have recalled such memories, I savour them afresh. I might even relive them before recording them in my journal in the form of words or phrases which capture the joy:

Tadpoles, the magnificent walk, the welcome we received in the restaurant, another good night's sleep, the variegated

greens of the countryside, the beckoning beach with its
turquoise sea, church bells summoning worshippers to
church.

'And what happens when you've had a lousy day?' someone once asked me when I was recommending this practice
at one of my Prayer Schools. I chuckled and suggested
in reply: 'The more lousy the day appears to have been,
the more important it is to do this prayer exercise.' On
dark days, when the future seems bleak and we feel
battered and bruised, it is easy to be beguiled into
believing that there is nothing for which to praise God.
But that assumption is usually far from the truth. On
such occasions, if we pause to look back in the way I
have described and home in on his gifts to us, we shall
see that the darkness has been spangled with pin-pricks of
light even though we may not have detected them when
they first began to twinkle.

On one such day, I struggled to recall tiny signs of
God's love and beauty. But when I paused to look back,
I recalled 'the dawn chorus, time to pour out my pain to
the God who cares, the kind invitation to the concert,
a wonderful sunny spring morning, the hedgehogs L gave
me, trees heavy with pink and white cherry blossom, a
cloudless slate-blue sky'. And I was forced to admit that
my seemingly dismal day had been punctuated with good
gifts which were in danger of being overlaid by gloom.
And, of course, the recognition of good gifts reminds us
of the presence of the Giver – God himself for, as James
puts it:

Every good and perfect gift is from above, coming down
from the Father of the heavenly lights, who does not
change like shifting shadows. (James 1:17)

Just as there is value in spending some five minutes each
day watching an action replay of the past twenty-four
hours and asking God to slow down the film when he

wants to remind us of the good gifts he has showered on us, so we can benefit enormously from watching that same video for a second time. Again, we set aside some five minutes. This time, the aim is to invite God to show us where he has been active in us. I sometimes liken this to taking a walk around the garden of our life in the presence of God. We ask him to point out where the fruit produced by his Spirit has started to bud or mature in us or, conversely, where weeds threaten to gain a stranglehold. This walk is always an adventure in the sense that we can never predict beforehand what God will point out. Sometimes the experience is deeply moving and at other times challenging.

Sometimes it is moving because God shows us where, by his grace, the love, joy, peace, patience, kindness and self-control Paul mentions in Galatians 5:22 has been offered by us to others, thus enriching their lives or bringing them comfort or peace. At other times, he will highlight occasions where we have been enabled by him to do things which, in our own strength, we would be incapable of achieving. He does this by bringing to the surface of our memory occasions when we have been uncharacteristically kind or patient, or moments when what we have said or done has clearly been inspired by him; or times when he has prompted us to pray for someone just when they most needed it. Such memories are humbling. They show us that, even though we were not aware of it at the time, God was present to us and in us. They draw from us gratitude that the Spirit of Jesus continues to transform us.

At other times we may find God focussing on far less attractive, even ugly, parts of our day. Frequently, for example, he will point out a particular mood – like irritability. And I have learned that when this happens I must not confess too quickly. To do that would be like plucking the leaves off a weed rather than digging it up by its roots. No. Instead, I must ask myself, 'What was it that gave rise to the irritability?'

I remember asking this question on one occasion and discovering that my irritability stemmed from a conversation I had had with a woman who seemed to talk at me rather than to me and I had become more and more bad-tempered even though I did not, I think, convey this frustration to her.

'Your attitude needs to change,' God seemed to whisper. 'You still need to grow in your ability to accept and love people just as they are.' This home truth was lovingly given and I admitted that it was all too accurate. And this resulted in repentance, not just of a few moments of impatience, but of something much deeper: the self-centredness which would keep at arm's length one of God's people who hurts so much that she feels she has to talk at people to conceal her pain.[1]

Reflection

Close your eyes. Think back to this time yesterday. Now watch an action replay of the past twenty-four hours. As the video plays on the screen of your mind, focus only on the good things that happened to you. Relish them. Relive them. Enjoy them all over again. Then, recognising them for what they are, good gifts from a good God, signs of his presence in your life, thank him in a verbal or a written prayer. Or simply jot down words or phrases to remind you of his goodness:

Think of a time when, most days, you can snatch between three and five minutes to do this exercise: in your lunch break maybe, or as you wake up or fall asleep, or as you travel to work. Write down some possibilities and then weigh up the pros and cons of using this particular time:

Now close your eyes again and watch an action replay of the same twenty-four-hour period. This time ask God to show you where he was active in your life even though you didn't recognise it. Let him point out where, by his grace, you allowed his Spirit to work through you and where, for various reasons, you missed an opportunity to act in a Christ-like way. Don't embark on a guilt trip or a cycle of self-congratulation. Simply be aware of ways in which God has been present to you. Again, jot down one or two words or phrases to remind you of what you have been shown. Then ask God to continue to work in you today:

2

At life's crossroads

Reading: Revelation 3:20

'Look at me. I stand at the door. I knock. If you hear me call and open the door, I'll come right in and sit down to supper with you.'[1]

'You can't sit on the fence for ever. Unless you choose Jesus as the Lord of your life, by implication you are rejecting him,' challenged the evangelist. He went on to explain that Jesus longs that we should surrender our entire lives to him and urged anyone who had never done so to 'make a decision' for Christ.

I had never heard anyone give that challenge before. But it made sense. If Jesus loved me enough to die for me, the least I could do was to express my thanks in an act of glad surrender. The surge of emotions that welled up inside me expressed more eloquently than any words the deepest desire of my heart and mind – for both were fully engaged in that moment – to place my life once and for all in the hands of the living God.

When the evangelist later invited those who would like to make such a commitment to Christ to come forward to

the front of the church, I pushed my way past my friend
who was sitting at the end of the pew, and stumbled up
the aisle. I knew what I wanted to do and was determined
to go through with this public abandonment of all I had
and all I was to the Christ who had revealed himself to
me afresh that night. That moment was a turning-point
in my life: a conversion experience. I meant every word
of the hymn we sang:

Just as I am, without one plea
But that Thy blood was shed for me,
And that Thou bidst me come to Thee,
O Lamb of God, I come.

Just as I am, though tossed about
With many a conflict, many a doubt,
Fightings and fears within, without,
O Lamb of God, I come.

Just as I am, Thou wilt receive,
Wilt welcome, pardon, cleanse, relieve,
Because Thy promise I believe,
O Lamb of God, I come.

Just as I am (Thy love unknown
Has broken every barrier down),
Now to be Thine, yea, Thine alone,
O Lamb of God, I come.

Just as I am, of that free love
The breadth, length, depth and height to prove,
Here for a season, then above –
O Lamb of God, I come.

(Charlotte Elliott)

After the service I struggled to express to my friend a
fraction of the relief and strange joy with which I seemed
to be inebriated. I had no name for the experience. I could
not claim that I had heard about Jesus for the first time
and that, *eureka*! I had fallen in love with him. It was

more like an underlining in ink of what had already been
written on my heart in pencil: the love for Christ which
had been instilled in me as a child. But it was liberating
and life-changing none the less.[2]

Reflection

Trace your own faith journey, perhaps by drawing a map
showing the way you have travelled thus far. Mark in some
of the crossroad experiences you have encountered along
the way:

God makes it clear in Revelation 2:4 that it is tragically
easy to lose our first love. 'Do you have any idea how far
you've fallen?' he asks.[3] Revelation 3:20 shows us one
way of turning back; of recovering our 'dear early love'.[4]
This invitation never fails to reassure me that no matter
how lukewarm or inattentive or lacking in openness I may
have become, God is still there – waiting. All I have to
do is to open up to him and he will come to me with the
warmth and closeness which is implied in that picture of
two people sitting side by side over a special and intimate
meal. And, as Basil Pennington points out, 'we won't sit
with a table between us. It will be "side by side" – like
the beloved disciple who could lean over and rest his head

upon his Master's bosom.'[5] Reflect on the mystery of this
love for as many minutes as you can.

Using your God-given imagination in the way God clearly
intended when he gave John this picture, see Jesus
standing outside the front door of your home. Listen to
his knock. Watch yourself as you respond to that knock.
Knowing that it is Jesus, do you hurry to open the door
with a warm welcome? Or do you open it reluctantly,
fearfully, begrudgingly? Notice how you invite him in.
Are you glad to have him in your home or embarrassed?
Take him on a conducted tour of your house. Watch
your own reaction and his as you show him one room
at a time. Are there rooms or cupboards or nooks and
crannies into which you hope he will not even peep, let
alone gaze? Trace your anxiety or embarrassment to its
source. Why would you prefer to hide this part of your
home from him?

When the conducted tour is completed, settle down and
talk to Jesus about your findings. Let him show you any
reasons why you have lost your first love. Ask him to
rekindle it. Ask him to show you any changes you need
to make in attitude or lifestyle so that your first love can
be restored and you can enjoy intimacy with him.

Write the prayer of your heart which has been born out
of the experience of these reflections:

3

In stillness

Reading: Psalm 63:1–8

O God, you are my God,
earnestly I seek you;
my soul thirsts for you,
my body longs for you,
in a dry and weary land
where there is no water.
I have seen you in the sanctuary
and beheld your power and your glory.
Because your love is better than life,
my lips will glorify you.
I will praise you as long as I live,
and in your name I will lift up my hands.
My soul will be satisfied as with the richest of foods;
with singing lips my mouth will praise you.
On my bed I remember you;
I think of you through the watches of the night.
Because you are my help,
I sing in the shadow of your wings.
My soul clings to you;
your right hand upholds me.

Whenever I could I would go to Mount St Bernard Abbey to pray. Sometimes all I could spare would be a few hours. Sometimes, I managed to stay for a whole day. Very occasionally I would make a retreat of thirty-six hours. What was it that drew me? A recent visit helped me to pin-point the power of the place. I had driven through hazardous conditions to reach the abbey, along snow-packed lanes, through a blinding blizzard; on the way my car had skidded and in doing so had collided with another, bigger car. Even so, when eventually I had parked outside the abbey guest house, picked my way through ankle-deep snowdrifts and lifted the latch of the oak chapel door, I became aware of a peace invading my spirit.

The hush of the prayer-saturated chapel seeped into me. Within seconds, I had fallen to my knees, aware of my surroundings, the smell of fresh furniture polish, the sound of the monks shuffling into the choir stalls, the wind howling round the building, yet intensely aware of a love which drew me to itself, the love of God. The sense of God's presence and love was so strong that it banished all memories of the traumatic journey. This love called from me a response. While the monks worshipped, like a sponge which had lain hard and shrivelled I opened every cell and fibre of my being to the warmth, the radiance and beckoning of the love of the living Lord.

'And this was how it always was,' I reflected. 'In this place the Lord calls me from my preoccupation with self and my overbusyness to focus on him and him only. In this place he touches me, the real me which often I hide from the world. He touches me through the winsomeness of the music, he touches me through the visual stimulus of the cross, he touches me through the powerful, prayerful atmosphere, he touches me through the flickering candle which somehow stills my harassed heart.'

When the monks left the church, I would linger there, as I did on this occasion. And I would be aware that every part of my being – body, mind and spirit – were open, attentive to the divine presence. I had done nothing to prepare myself for this eventuality: God had done it. The initiative was his. The miracle was his. By beaming his love on to me in a way I could feel, parts of me which normally remain closed, unfolded. I suppose I was rather like the water-lily which opens itself when it can bask in warm sunshine but which closes its petals when cloud or rain obliterate the sun.

What I heard in those times of listening was more than a voice: it was a presence. Yes. I heard the Lord call my name. But I also 'heard' his tenderness. I soaked up his love. And this listening was on a level which runs deeper than mere words. Sometimes it seemed as though Jesus himself stood in front of me or beside me or above me. This encounter with him overwhelmed me. Was it his radiance? Was it the tenderness of his gaze? Or was it the fact of his gaze? The only way I can describe it is to liken it to the overwhelming a person feels when they love someone very deeply. That person's heart burns with pure pleasure at the joy of being in the presence of the loved one, that person's eyes sparkle or shine or mist over with warmth and deep-felt emotion, but that person does not speak. No words are necessary. They might even prove intrusive for they could trivialise the love. And nothing must spoil the ecstasy of their encounter which may be all too brief in any case. They are content simply 'to be' in one another's presence. But that silence is packed with warm communication.[1]

Reflection

Busyness can create the kind of barrenness the Psalmist describes at the beginning of Psalm 63. Stillness, on the other hand, gives us the opportunity to tune in to God's outpoured love. Notice when the Psalmist felt

God's presence and love. Compare this with your own experience. When, realistically, can you carve out quiet for God? In addition to your daily 'twenty minutes with God', can you earmark an hour on one of your weekly days off, a morning or an equivalent each month and perhaps an annual retreat? Take out your diary or your calendar and plot these dates into it now. Or jot down some possibilities here:

Notice what the Psalmist writes about God's love. Do you agree? If so, always approach your prayer place with reverence and awe expecting to be encountered by the God of love. Tune in to his presence. Let his love refresh and renew you. Spend most of your prayer time allowing this to happen if necessary.

It sometimes takes people a long time to establish a realistic prayer rhythm so be patient and take heart from the following observation:

> *All your love, your stretching out, your hope, your thirst,*
> *God is creating in you so that he may fill you. It is not*
> *your desire that makes it happen, but his. He longs*
> *through your heart . . . In your prayer God is seeking*
> *you and himself creating the prayer; he is on the inside*
> *of the longing . . . God's longing for us is the spring of*
> *ours for him.*[2]

'God is on the inside of the longing . . .' Tell God how you react to that claim.

4

When busy

Reading: Psalm 34:1–9
I will extol the Lord at all times;
his praise will always be on my lips,
My soul will boast in the Lord;
let the afflicted hear and rejoice.
Glorify the Lord with me:
let us exalt his name together.
I sought the Lord, and he answered me;
he delivered me from all my fears.
Those who look to him are radiant;
their faces are never covered with shame.
This poor man called, and the Lord heard him;
he saved him out of all his troubles . . .
Taste and see that the Lord is good;
blessed is the man who takes refuge in him.
Fear the Lord, you his saints,
for those who fear him lack nothing.

Brother Lawrence, author of a little gem called *The Practice of the Presence of God*, used to encourage people to talk to God about everything – to seek his help before attempting even the most mundane task. When *he* was about to begin work, he would simply ask God to give him the grace both to apply his mind to the task in hand *and* to continue in God's felt presence. He asked, too, that God would assist him, accept his work as a love offering and continue to captivate his affections. Having prayed such a prayer, he opened himself to receive the strength he needed 'and more besides'.

But does this system work for us today, in our busy, frenetic, materialistic society? I asked myself this question while my husband and I were leading a retreat overseas. We would meet the retreatants as a group each morning, discover together the riches of Bible meditation, then each individual would spend time pondering a passage of scripture on their own. Later that morning individuals would meet with David or myself to share with us the fruit of their prayer time.

One of my retreatants had undertaken to cook lunch for all of us so I used to meet with her first. As soon as she left me, I knew that she would be busy working in the kitchen and so I felt anxious lest her busyness should spoil her stillness with God. With this in mind, I used to pray with her before she left me that, like Brother Lawrence, she would be as aware of the presence of God while cooking as she was when she was meditating in her own room.

One day, I asked her whether being the cook was interrupting her retreat. She looked surprised by my question and replied with a genuine: 'Oh no! While I'm preparing the lunch, I talk to the Lord and he carries on talking to me.'

So on the day when the dishwasher failed, the telephone went dead and the car refused to start, she still found herself held in the peace which was pervading every part of her being as she meditated and prayed. 'I talk to the Lord about all these things,' she said 'and I know that he is there helping me.'

Pray while you work

Brother Lawrence also encouraged his retreatants to pray in the middle of the maelstrom. Hc confessed that, at such times, he simply prayed a prayer like, 'Lord, I cannot do this unless you enable me.'

Down the centuries, countless Christians have testified to the difference such prayer makes to the pressures they face. When they pray, instead of becoming knotted up, like Martha (Luke 10:40), they expect to see evidence of God's presence in their workplace.

I think, for example, of Jackie Pullinger. In *Crack in the Wall*, she describes how, at first, she was besieged by a sense of helplessness when faced with the stench and corruption of the Walled City – a particularly sordid part of Hong Kong. The surrounding tenements, the twelve-year-old prostitutes, the thousands of poor forced to live in one-room dwellings, the gangs and the opium dens both distressed her and drew from her a compassion which reflected the compassion of Christ and gave birth to a question: how could she even begin to pray for the inhabitants of this place? At first she felt defeated:[1]

> *Then I learned that praying in tongues was to help people when they did not know how to pray or had run out of words. Desperate by this time to see evidence of God's power in action I began to pray privately in tongues for the dying in the Walled City. After about six weeks . . . extraordinary things began to happen . . . I lost count of the number of changed lives around me.*[2]

Reflection

Write your own version of the kind of prayer Brother Lawrence used to pray before beginning a new task:

Write your own version of the kind of prayer he used to pray in the middle of the maelstrom taking some of these 'arrow prayers' as a model maybe:

> *Lord, don't let me think I can cope by myself and won't need you. (John Donne)*

> *Holy Spirit, think through me 'till your ideas are my ideas. (Amy Carmichael)*

> *Lord, help me to believe that you are good, even when bad things happen. (Lady Jane Grey in the Tower of London)*

Tell God what makes it difficult for you to do what the Psalmist did: to extol him *at all times*.

5

Through creation

Reading: Psalm 19:1–4

The heavens declare the glory of God;
the skies proclaim the work of his hands.
Day after day they pour forth speech;
night after night they display knowledge.
There is no speech or language
where their voice is not heard.
Their voice goes out into all the earth,
their words to the ends of the world . . .

How often, I wonder, has a star-spangled sky or a stunning sunset, a sunrise or sun-pierced storm clouds become, for someone in need, the smile of God? But God smiles not just through the splendour of the sky, he smiles through the whole of his creation: the heavens and the earth in all their vast array. This, surely, is implied through that recurring refrain which punctuates the first chapter of Genesis: 'And God saw that it was good.'

I once meditated on Genesis 2:2 – the sequel to Genesis 1: 'By the seventh day God had finished the work he had been doing; so on the seventh day he rested.' I imagined

God standing and surveying all that he had made: light and darkness, water and sky, trees and plants, sun, moon and stars, birds and animals, fish and colourful sea corals. I seemed to see him standing and staring, savouring and smiling, certain that everything that he had made was not simply satisfactory. It was good. Very good. Perfect. I seemed to see, too, how the Creator smiled as he created his masterpieces – the first man and first woman.

But it was some years later, when praying with clay in my hands, that I sensed I understood a little more of how God might have felt about this world he had created. I was praying with a group of friends. We had each been given a lump of clay which we worked while someone read verses of scripture comparing our lives to lumps of clay in the heavenly potter's hands:

We are the clay, you are the potter; we are all the work of your hand.
(Isaiah 64:8)

Like clay in the hand of the potter, so are you in my hand.
(Jeremiah 18:6)

I was astonished to discover how quickly the crude, cold lump was warmed by the heat of my hands, how malleable it became and how I longed to make of it something beautiful. I pummelled it and rolled it, squeezed it and moulded it until, at last, I created a small dish with a scalloped edge. By that time it belonged to me even though it had an identity all its own. I held it in reverence. And when someone suggested that we might end the evening by placing the objects we had made back into the sack of raw clay, a wave of protest swept over me. 'I couldn't bear to do that, it's special.'

And it was special to me because I had created it. I placed it on a window sill and, for days, would finger it affectionately. Others in the group confessed to similar feelings of attachment for the objects they had made. It underlined just how precious to God each of us is; how precious, too, is each particle of his creation. Was that why Jesus encouraged us to listen to the language of nature? 'Contemplate the lilies,' he says. Look at them, feel them, smell them. Examine the blades of grass that grow in the meadow. Even Solomon's most ornate, royal robes could not compare with the splendour with which God clothes these seemingly commonplace parts of his creation.[1]

What Jesus seems to be saying here is: let creation give you a glimpse of God's glory and faithfulness – that just as authors come to us through the books they write, so God visits us through the things he creates. Paul puts it this way:

> *Christ is the exact likeness of the unseen God. He existed before God made anything at all and, in fact, Christ himself is the Creator who made everything in heaven and earth, the things we can see and the things we can't. He was before all else began and it is his power that holds everything together. (Colossians 1:15–17)*

I was turning the phrase, 'In him all things hold together' over and over in my mind while I was walking along a deserted beach on one occasion. As I did so, the parts of creation before me – the sea and the mountains, the vineyards and the orchards, the sky and the luscious green fields, took on new meaning. They were no longer simply objects which Jesus had made, they were also expressions of beauty which still respond to his orchestration. 'It is as though Jesus, like a skilful conductor, continues to wave his baton, drawing from his handiwork a symphony of praise,' I thought as I listened to the music of the waves lapping the shore, as I watched them break in a frothing, foaming mass and as I felt the breeze and the sun warming my face.[2]

Reflection

What do you understand by the Psalmist's claim:

The heavens declare the glory of God;
the skies proclaim the work of his hands.
Day after day they pour forth speech.
Their voice goes out into all the earth,

In Romans 1, Paul makes this claim:

Since the creation of the world God's invisible qualities
– his eternal power and divine nature – have been clearly
seen, being understood from what has been made.

In other words the Creator reveals himself through the things that he has created: the night sky, the exotic bird, the calm sea and the howling gale, crocuses piercing layers of ice and snow, bronze bracken in autumn, rain-bearing thunder-clouds. So Carlo Carretto invites us to 'contemplate what lies before you. It is God's way of making himself present.'

Walk around with your eyes and ears open today. Expect God to come to you through his creation. He may speak through one tiny flower, or he may reveal his suffering to you through the way his wonderful world is being abused. Perhaps a tiny bud or a new-born baby will become a symbol of new life and new hope.

Think of a colour. Then look for that colour as you pass people's gardens or window-boxes or as you drive through the countryside. Ask yourself, 'What kind of Being must he be who created colour?' Or look at shapes and ask: 'What kind of Being must he be who created shapes?' Make a note of the thoughts that came to you:

Think of the complexity of our world and what it takes to orchestrate the whole of creation. Throughout the day, repeat the phrase: Jesus holds all this together. Then write a prayer expressing how you feel about the One who holds all things together:

6

On waking

Reading: Lamentations 3:22–6

Because of the Lord's great love we are not consumed,
for his compassions never fail.
They are new every morning: great is your faithfulness.
I say to myself, 'The Lord is my portion; therefore I will
wait for him.'
The Lord is good to those whose hope is in him,
   to the one who seeks him;
it is good to wait quietly for the salvation of the Lord.

One way of coming to God is to take advantage of life's 'little solitudes', to borrow Richard Foster's phrase – those early morning moments in bed before the family wakes up or before we know we have to get up, that cup of coffee in the middle of the morning, sitting in bumper-to-bumper traffic during the rush hour, travelling by train or by car, queuing in the supermarket: snippets of time I once heard dubbed 'Kingdom moments'. We can train ourselves to sense the presence of the indwelling Christ in such moments just as Mary did when God's Son was forming in her womb:

> *She who began by enclosing God within her womb,*
> *herself needs no enclosure . . . Hers the busy day*
> *of cooking, washing, sweeping, shopping at the noisy*
> *bazaar, sewing, mending, nursing, but through it all,*
> *the awe-inspiring love-union with the Lord.[1]*

Commuters and journalists, politicians and film pro-
ducers, pilots and firemen, office workers and social
workers and others whose work-day is notoriously stress-
ful might envy Mary and question whether there are
many 'Kingdom moments' in their day. There are. The
challenge comes to each of us to recognise them as George
Sinker emphasises in his book *Jesus Loved Martha*. He
encourages his readers, for example, to remind themselves
of two verses of scripture when they wake up: 'Get up and
pray' (Luke 22:46) and 'Very early in the morning, while
it was still dark, Jesus got up, left the house and went off
to a solitary place, where he prayed' (Mark 1:35).

> *It is Jesus who comes and wakes you, by whatever means*
> *He uses, and invites you to spend the first moment of the*
> *day with Him. Why? From His point of view, because He*
> *loves you and desires your company. From your point of*
> *view, because He knows it will be another tiring day and*
> *He wants to pour into you the strength and courage, the*
> *patience and peace to face each test the day will bring.[2]*

Or again, he suggests that when we use the bathroom
we turn our mind to Jesus and the man at the Pool of
Siloam (John 9:7). 'Go, wash,' Jesus said to this man.
And Sinker adds:

> *Jesus bids us wash. But washing to him always signified*
> *the sacrament of a clean heart. Washing in the Bible is a*
> *double action, bodily and spiritual. If we were to form*
> *the habit of thought, we would come consciously into His*
> *presence every time we washed, receiving the cleansing*
> *of His forgiveness and reunion with Him.[3]*

And we would use the prayer of the Psalmist: 'Wash me and I shall be whiter than snow' (Psalm 51:7).

Dressing is another activity which can so easily be combined with prayer. Recall Romans 13:14, suggests George Sinker: 'Clothe yourselves with the Lord Jesus Christ.' To be clothed with Christ means to be clothed with 'His beauty, His strength, His love, His understanding, His patience, His peace, His joy. There is no end to the glory of this garment which He offers you to put on first thing every day.'[4]

Even the washing-up can remind us of Jesus's promises and presence if we recall Jesus's command, 'Clean the inside of the cup and dish' (Matthew 23:26). As we clean the dishes or load the dish-washer we can pray the Psalmist's prayer: 'Create in me a pure heart, O God, and renew a steadfast spirit within me' (Psalm 51:10).

This way, just as St Teresa found God so easily among the pots and pans and just as Brother Lawrence learned how to cast the occasional loving gaze at God when elbow-deep in potato peelings, so we will find that even a kitchen can become a haven if we tune in to the sound of God's silence no matter what is going on around us.[5]

Long before George Sinker penned this advice, Celtic Christians were encountering God in the way he pre-scribed. They perceived God as the One who pervaded everything so they expected to encounter him in their workplace and on their travels. Their prayers reveal that their senses were like antennae – ever alert and ready to detect the presence of the all-powerful, invis-ible One whom they expected to meet when fishing or farming, dressing or eating, waking or falling asleep. They assumed and gave thanks for his presence at the birth of their babies and rested in the confidence that he would still be with them in the moment of death. He was real. That is why they could produce delightful prayers for every imaginable occasion. Like this compre-hensive one:

God in all
  In your walking – God
  In your talking – God
  In your life – God
  In your strife – God
  In your seeing – God
  In your being – God
  In your days – God
  In your ways – God
  In your night – God
  In your plight – God
  In your reason – God
  In every season – God
  With God I'm bound
  All around.[6]

Reflection

As you lie in bed, wondering whether to get up, recognise that God has not left you while you have been sleeping. He is there, in the bedroom with you. Open yourself to him. Even though you may not be able to feel his presence, be aware that he is there loving and strengthening and supporting you as you prepare to face the challenge of this new day. Remind yourself that he loves you, he accepts you just as you are, he will be with you every step of the way today.

Eric Milner-White, one-time Dean of York Minster, wrote a prayer called 'On Waking':

O Lord, when I awake, the day begins,
waken me to your Presence;
waken me to your indwelling;
waken me to inward sight of you,

and speech with you,
and strength from you;
that all my earthly walk may waken into song
and my spirit leap up to you all day,
all ways.[7]

Use this prayer or write a prayer of your own which you can learn to use on waking:

Think ahead. When might you find some 'Kingdom Moments' today? Even if those moments are fleeting, pause to remind yourself that you are still enfolded in God's love. He is still there for you, strengthening and supporting you. Thank him.

7

While sleeping

Reading: Matthew 2:13–15; 19–20

*An angel of the Lord appeared to Joseph in a dream.
'Get up,' he said, 'take the child and his mother and
escape to Egypt. Stay there until I tell you, for Herod
is going to search for the child to kill him.'*

*So he got up, took the child and his mother during the
night and left for Egypt, where he stayed until the death
of Herod. And so was fulfilled what the Lord had said
through the prophet: 'Out of Egypt I called my son' . . .
After Herod died, an angel of the Lord appeared in a
dream to Joseph in Egypt and said, 'Get up, take the
child and his mother and go to the land of Israel, for
those who were trying to take the child's life are dead.'*

The book of Numbers implies that visions and dreams are
perfectly valid means of prophetic revelations: 'When a
prophet of the Lord is among you, I reveal myself to him
in visions, I speak to him in dreams' (Numbers 12:6).
I found that Jeremiah endorses the fact that a prophet
might receive a prophetic dream: 'Let the prophet who
has a dream tell his dream' (Jeremiah 23:28).

Jeremiah himself records such a dream in which God describes the peace and harmony and obedience which he will bestow on his chosen people (Jeremiah 31:26). And Joel foresees the day when God's Spirit will be poured out on all mankind and when the links between prophecy, dreams and visions will be crystal clear:

I will pour out my Spirit on all people.
Your sons and daughters will prophesy,
*   your old men will dream dreams,*
*   your young men will see visions.*
(Joel 2:28 quoted Acts 2:17)

Dreams also feature frequently in the New Testament.
With this data in front of me, I began to reflect on a vivid dream I had had on the last day of a sun-splashed holiday in Greece one spring. With David and Kevin and Christina, our children, I had shoe-horned myself into the cabin of the passenger boat which plies between the island of Rhodes and Athens. We had torn ourselves away from the delights of Lindos with its tiny harbour, its cobbled streets, its colourful bazaars and its famous donkey transport. After the night voyage, we would collect our dormobile and start the long haul home by road.

That night my sleep was disturbed by a dream in which I saw our dormobile being towed away by a lorry. The vehicle was a total wreck. In the dream, I watched the rescue lorry disappear from sight taking most of our possessions with it. I woke from that dream, lay in the darkness and, with uncharacteristic calm, prayed: 'Lord, if that should happen to us, please give me the courage to cope.' The prayer offered, with a peace which does not match my personality, I fell asleep.

On the following day, in high spirits, I drove from Athens to Skopje in what was then Yugoslavia. There I handed over the driving to my husband. The dream forgotten, I settled on the back seat of the dormobile to read the map and relax. I don't know what made me glance up at my husband. What I do remember is the grim, grey look on his face as I watched him juggle with a steering wheel which clearly was out of control. With incredulity, I watched him drive through mid-air and head for a silver-birch tree. I heard my nine-year-old daughter scream, 'No! No!' and I felt the dormobile bounce off the trunk of the tree before somersaulting down the steep embankment.

Some minutes later, I lay on the grassy bank, conscious of a dull pain between my shoulder blades, aware of blood pouring from a head wound and staring at the twisted machinery before me which six months earlier had been our brand-new, blue Volkswagen dormobile. But I was not surprised. Nor shaken. It was as though I had lived this moment the night before in my dream. This was simply an action replay of a familiar event. Through the trauma of the chaotic days which followed, my heart stayed at peace.

Two days later, while I lay in a primitive hospital north of Skopje wearing a crown of bandages on my injured head, a lorry towed the dormobile containing most of our possessions to the scrap heap – just as my dream had foretold. While I was regaining strength in this hospital, news filtered through that my father had died tragically and suddenly of a heart attack. By the time we reached home, the funeral was over. I was never able to say my final farewell to him.

My husband referred to the accident and the bereavement and the dream in a sermon on one occasion soon after we arrived back in England. A surgeon happened to be in the congregation that morning. After the service, he told my husband something we had not appreciated at the time: that if someone was to suffer the kind of head injuries I sustained and be so quickly subjected to the added pain of bereavement, this dream was the kindest possible preparation they could have. The trust the dream engendered ensured that, at the time of the tragedies, I was relaxed, conscious that I was held by a love that would not let me go.

I marvelled at God's faithfulness and treasured this memory with its hidden message of love, constancy and compassion.[1]

Reflection

Think of occasions recorded in the New Testament when God spoke to his people through dreams. Would you agree that, at least in Bible times, one significant way in which God revealed himself to people was through dreams?

Are you aware of God ever coming to you through the symbolic imagery of a dream? If so, recall the incident. If not, meditate on the way God appeared to Joseph in his dream. Record how you feel about a God who uses the night hours, when we are relaxed and strangely attentive, to speak into our situation:

Often, when we dream, the person speaking to us is not God, it is ourselves. That does not mean that the dream is unimportant. Often, if we stop to reflect on and pray over them, these dreams will also show us facts and feelings which we do not have time to face or which we are unwilling to face while we are awake. There is therefore value in recording our dreams. I find it helpful to follow these guidelines:

Write down the dream using the first person present tense as though the dream is still unfolding:

'I am watching our wrecked dormobile being towed away by a lorry.'

Give the dream a title to help you locate it some time in the future when it might make more sense than now. *What title would you give Joseph's two dreams? And what title would you give my dream?*

Try to discern the precise theme of the dream. *What would you say was the theme of Joseph's dream? What was the theme of my dream?*

Write down the effect the dream had on you. *What effect did Joseph's dreams have on him; and what effect did my dream have on me:*

Does the dream ask you a question like:

Is there something in this dream that I need to face?
Is there a message here that I need to receive and act upon?
What needs to be done and how am I going to do it?

Tell God how you feel about this invitation to take your dreams seriously, to listen to yourself and to him speaking to you through them.

8

Through the implanted Word

Reading: Matthew 13:3–9; 18–23

Jesus said: 'A farmer went out to sow his seed. As he was scattering the seed, some fell along the path, and the birds came and ate it up. Some fell on rocky places, where it did not have much soil. It sprang up quickly, because the soil was shallow. But when the sun came up, the plants were scorched, and they withered because they had no root. Other seed fell among thorns, which grew up and choked the plants. Still other seed fell on good soil, where it produced a crop – a hundred, sixty or thirty times what was sown. He who has ears, let him hear . . .

'Listen then to what the parable of the sower means: When anyone hears the message about the kingdom and does not understand it, the evil one comes and snatches away what was sown in his heart. This is the seed sown along the path. The one who received the seed that fell on rocky places is the man who hears the word and at once receives it with joy. But since he has no root, he lasts only a short time. When trouble or persecution comes because of the word, he quickly falls away. The one who received the seed that fell among the thorns is the man who hears the word, but the worries of this life and the deceitfulness of wealth choke it, making it unfruitful. But the one who received the seed that fell on good soil is the man who hears the word and understands it. He produces a crop, yielding a hundred, sixty or thirty times what was sown.'

In the parable of the sower, Jesus shows how his Word needs to find a home . . . in the soil of our lives so that it can germinate and grow. Equally, he reminds us: 'If you make my word your home you will learn the truth and the truth will make you free (John 8:31–2 JB).

The Bible speaks of a three-pronged truth: the truth is revelation in the form of a person, Jesus; the truth is revelation in the form of a 'letter from home', the Bible; and the truth is God's Word applied to our individual situation by the enlightenment of God's agent of truth, his Holy Spirit, so that God's truth becomes enfleshed.[1]

One of the reasons why I enjoy living in the Middle East is that the countryside near my home is so much like Palestine. As I walk, therefore, I frequently sense the coming together of those three expressions of the Word. But that is not new. Many pages of my prayer journal remind me of the way God has put his finger on areas of my life and shown how they cripple me or distort his image.

I once expressed in my journal hatred of someone who had hurt me. God challenged me. The real reason for the hatred was that my pride had been wounded because friendship with me was a lower priority on this person's list than it used to be. God forced me, too, to face my jealousy. 'Pride and jealousy are sins to be confessed,' the Holy Spirit seemed to whisper, 'not rights to cling on to.' He gave me no peace until this sinful rubble was tipped out at the foot of the cross.

Sometimes the changes God wanted to bring about in my life took years rather than minutes. During a difficult stage of my marriage, whole pages of my prayer journal were devoted to the anger and frustration which poisoned my life and which stemmed from the growing tensions between my husband and myself. In prayer I would whine to God about David. In prayer I would throw down the gauntlet and challenge God to change my husband so that the quality of our marriage could improve. In prayer I would pour out the self-pity that filled me to the brim. And in prayer, God would come to me, hear me out, absorb my bitterness, touch my bruised and battered heart, and gently but persistently show me, not where David needed to change, but where *I* must change. Comments like this recur in my journal:

> *And yes! I hear your voice again. Forgive! Not just seven times but seventy times seven.*[2]

And I recall an occasion where, once again, I was eaten up by bitterness and resentment and fell to blaming and criticising my husband until, one morning, while I was talking to God about my pain, an all-too-familiar verse of scripture burst into my awareness with such clarity it was as though Jesus himself stood beside me whispering:

> *Why do you look at the speck of sawdust in your brother's eye and pay no attention to the plank in your own eye? How can you say to your brother, 'Let me take the speck out of your eye,' when all the time there is a plank in your own eye? You hypocrite, first take the plank out of your own eye, and then you will see clearly to remove the speck from your brother's eye. (Matthew 7:3–5)*

That reminder was so apposite that it melted my bitterness and even gave birth to a smile – and a determination to examine myself to see where my perspective was warped. Such is the power of the Word spoken, applied and acted upon.

Is that why Jesus assumed that his followers would

possess a thorough working knowledge of the scriptures? Is that why, when lack of biblical insight blinded their eyes, Jesus rebuked them? (Luke 24:25–7). Isn't that why, in the desert, he confronts Satan face to face? With authority and poise, he withstands the enemy with one economical phrase: 'It is written . . .' (Luke 4:4,8).

For Jesus, as Jim Packer reminds us, 'it is written' was the end of the argument. 'There could be no appeal against the verdict of scripture for that would be to appeal against the judgement of God himself.'[3]

Reflection
And his that gentle voice we hear,
Soft as the breath of even,
That checks each fault and calms each fear
And speaks of heav'n.'

(*Harriet Auber 1773–1862*)

Think of occasions when God has come to you to challenge, rebuke or comfort you with a word of scripture which was implanted in you months, even years earlier. Recall how it felt at the time and remind yourself of the consequences.

Re-read Jesus's parable of the sower. Recall occasions when the seed of God's Word has been snatched away by the Evil One because you have failed to understand it. Have there been times when, because of crises or criticisms, the seed of God's Word has failed to take root in your life? When? What was the crisis or the criticism? Recall occasions when your spiritual growth was stunted because of an over-concern with wealth or worry. And ask God to show you times when your life has been like fertile soil and his Word has taken root inside you. Jot down some of your findings:

As you reflect on that parable today, how would you describe the field of your life?

Through Bible meditation

Reading: Ephesians 3: 14–21

I kneel before the Father, from whom his whole family in heaven and on earth derives its name. I pray that out of his glorious riches he may strengthen you with power through his Spirit in your inner being, so that Christ may dwell in your hearts through faith. And I pray that you, being rooted and established in love, may have power, together with all the saints, to grasp how wide and long and high and deep is the love of Christ, and to know this love that surpasses knowledge – that you may be filled to the measure of the fulness of God.

Now to him who is able to do immeasurably more than all we ask or imagine, according to his power that is at work within us, to him be glory in the church and in Christ Jesus throughout all generations, for ever and ever! Amen.

Love has to communicate itself. If they live apart, lovers spend hours talking on the telephone or writing letters to one another. They read those love letters several times – slowly savouring each sentence, seeing the smile behind the words, sensing the warmth no words can convey.

The message which throbs through the Bible is that God loves us like that. The writer of the book of Revelation sums it up in three words: 'God loves us' (3: 9). And his letters to us are concealed in the Bible. If we want to grasp the breadth and the length, the height and the depth of this love, the very best way to do it is to meditate on the mystery of his love as expressed in the scriptures. To savour it. A well-tried method of savouring the scriptures has been handed down to us from the fourth century and Christians today are rediscovering its value.

St John of the Cross links this method to Jesus's invitation, 'Ask and it will be given to you; seek and you will find; knock and the door will be opened' (Matthew 7: 7).

Seek in **Reading**
  and you will find in **Meditation**.
Knock in **Prayer**
  and it will be opened to you
  in **Contemplation**.

Reading

We begin this method of prayer by becoming still in the presence of God and by asking the Holy Spirit to shed his light on the words we read. We then read the passage several times until we are familiar with it. This activity, unlike much of our reading, is rather like attentive listening. It is concentrating, not so much on the words, as on the One who is speaking the words we read. And it is acknowledging that this message is inspired. In other words, our listening is laced with anticipation. We expect God to speak. When we read, we personalise the words, making them our own, welcoming in faith all we hear.

And just as lovers read between the lines and discover the unseen presence, the love and the smile on the face of the loved one, so we read between the lines of scripture, conscious that God is anxious to convey so much more than words can ever say.

Receiving
Two people who feel drawn to one another seek to deepen their relationship by spending time together, talking and listening to each other and finding out more and more about each other. Similarly, this second phase of savouring or praying the scriptures is designed to enable us to discover who this God of love really is and what he wants to show us. And just as, when we talk with a loved one, a certain phrase or sentence sometimes sticks in our minds so that we find ourselves turning it over for several days after the conversation has taken place, in a similar way fragments of God's Word lodge in our minds and beg to be chewed over. When we talk with a friend or relative, we do not stop to question why some of their words seem to possess a certain magnetic power; neither do we ask why certain phrases of the Bible have drawn us to themselves. We simply relish them by repeating them over and over again until we become aware that they are penetrating our entire being with the purity of the love of Jesus. This way we breathe in God's message of love and allow it to fill our spiritual lungs, to circulate round our entire beings, to permeate the whole of us. And this leads to the third phase of this prayer.

Responding
To return to the analogy of two lovers or two friends who are deepening their relationship, when one expresses affection or warmth, care or concern, it produces in the other a spontaneous reaction: a response of the heart. And that is what happens when we read God's Word slowly and meditatively. As a small portion from the Bible beckons us and we respond to it and to God, we might find our hearts leaping for joy at this fresh coming of God, or aching to know him better, being overwhelmed with awe or hungry to come even closer to him. Or we might hear his rebuke

and fall on our faces in repentance. Equally, we might find blinkers being removed from our eyes so that our vision of God expands and clarifies and we find ourselves rededicating ourselves to him in love. It is important to make sure that we give ourselves time in prayer, not simply to hear God but to respond to him in whatever way seems appropriate.

Resting

Finally, just as, when two people who love one another and feel comfortable with one another, learn to be content just 'to be' in each other's company, so we move into the phase of prayer where we are content to rest in God's loving presence. We focus, not on the words, and not on ourselves, but on God himself. And although we cannot see him because he is invisible, we act as though, with the eyes of faith, we do see him. We feel the fresh inflow of his love, absorb it, luxuriate in it and open ourselves to him to do in us and with us what he chooses.[1]

Reflection

Re-read, as slowly as possible, the verses from Ephesians with which we began. Read them in order to meditate on them in the way I have described above. Concentrate, not so much on the words, as on the love of the One they describe. Expect God to speak to you. Read slowly and meditatively until a word, a phrase or a sentence draws you to itself. When it does, lay down your book and turn those words over and over in your mind as its truth trickles

from your head into your heart. Now write the word or
words down:

When you have assimilated this fraction of God's Word
for several minutes, respond to it, telling God what kind of
an impact this fresh reminder of his love has made on you:
joy, bewilderment, assurance, an increase of reciprocal
love, fear, guilt:

As you go about the routine of your day, remind yourself
of 'your' word from God and continue to respond to it.
This way you will be aware that God comes to us all
through the day in the Word we have meditated on and
internalised.

10

Through the imagination

Reading: John 20:19–23

On the evening of that first day of the week, when the disciples were together with the doors locked for fear of the Jews, Jesus came and stood among them and, said 'Peace be with you!' After he said this, he showed them his hands and side. The disciples were overjoyed when they saw the Lord. And Jesus said, 'Peace be with you! As the Father has sent me, I am sending you.' And with that he breathed on them and said, 'Receive the Holy Spirit. If you forgive anyone his sins, they are forgiven; if you do not forgive them, they are not forgiven.'

When meditating on a gospel story like this, it can be helpful to picture the scene as vividly as possible and then, rather than simply gazing at the picture as though you were watching a video, to imagine that you are able to step into the scene and interact with the characters concerned.

I did this with this particular story on the first day of a retreat on one occasion. Using my imagination I stepped into the Upper Room where the disciples had locked themselves into their fear and grief, their shock and bewilderment. While I was there, I had the thrill of encountering the Risen Lord. With the ears of my heart, I heard his excited greeting: 'Shalom! Peace be with you!' Together with the disciples, I had held my breath as I gazed in adoration at his nail-pierced hands and wounded side. I had sensed the mood change in the disciples as joy percolated through their fear, turning their doubt to trust and faith, and I had taken off the sandals of my heart as Jesus drew near and breathed into me his Holy Spirit.

But then, it seemed as though the One who had blessed me so richly and undeservedly suddenly slapped me in the face by saying: 'If you forgive people's sins, they are forgiven; if you do not forgive them, they are not forgiven' (v. 23 GNB). The love which had welled up in my heart turned to anger and, when I left that Upper Room, I felt cheated and hurt. So I asked myself some pertinent questions. Why did that reference to forgiving others prick the bubble? Could it be that Jesus was putting his finger on something in my life which needed addressing rather urgently? And then the pain of months rushed from the hidden recesses of my heart where I had repressed it.

For months a colleague and I had been locked in conflict. We had worked hard to understand and love one another but all our efforts had failed. It seemed that we had only to be in one another's presence to hurt each other – by a look, a sentence or even a silence. So we had recoiled, stunned and bewildered. Now, it seemed, instead of giving me the reprieve I longed for on this week-long retreat, Jesus was encouraging me to re-open the closed file and do the prayer work without which lasting reconciliation would have been impossible.

That day, my journal recorded not messages of love but rather an outpouring of pain as I told the Lord how deeply I had felt wounded by this woman. I wrote pages explaining why I felt unable to forgive. In doing this, it was as though an abscess was lanced and the pus of bitterness and hatred burst from me on to the unwitting

page of my journal. Even when I had completed this
diatribe, I confessed that I still felt unable or unwilling
to forgive but I added a tentative request: 'Give me the
grace to be willing to be made willing to let go of the hurt
and hatred: to forgive.'

Next day, I returned, in my meditation, to the same
verse: 'If you forgive people's sins, they are forgiven; if
you do not forgive them, they are not forgiven.' In my
imagination I returned, too, to the Upper Room where,
again, I heard Jesus saying to the disciples and to me:
'Look at my hands. Look at my side.' This time, I
not only looked, I crept up to Jesus and placed my
finger in the hole in his hand and slipped my hand
into the wound in his side. These wounds reminded
me of the brutality of his death – the price he was
prepared to pay so that my many failures might be
forgiven.

Slowly, my defences crumbled like chalk. Looking into
my Redeemer's eyes, I was able to pray with integrity
the prayer he taught us to pray: 'Forgive us our sins as
we forgive those who have sinned against us.' I knew
that he understood the full implications of this prayer.
I knew, too, that not only had this Bible meditation set
my colleague free from the emotional corner into which I
had pushed her, but that I had also been set free from the
poison which had been pulsating around my entire being,
polluting me and many other relationships.

I would have preferred to have begun my retreat on a
much cosier, more comforting note but the purpose of
Bible meditation is not necessarily to bring us comfort,
though so often it does do that. It is to bring us into
an encounter with the God who sometimes deems it
necessary to help us clear away the obstacles which bar
us from enjoying the intimacy he so much wants us to
enjoy; who sometimes discerns that ever deeper levels
of our personality need his healing, liberating touch so
that we can enjoy the wholeness into which he is always
leading us.[1]

Reflection

Some Christians seem very fearful of using their imagination. They somehow seem to think that, while God gave them a mind, Satan gave birth to their imagination. But think, for a moment, about the way Jesus taught both the well-educated of his day as well as the illiterate. He told them parables, stories. So when he was asked a philosophical question by a lawyer: 'Who is my neighbour?' he refrained from giving a three-point sermon. He told a story about a man who was mugged on the notorious Jerusalem to Jericho road. At the end of the story, they were not only spell-bound but informed. Yet Jesus did not apply the story. The story *was* the theology. By entering into it, they could all answer the question, 'Who is my neighbour?'

Ask God to put you back in touch with his wonderful gift of the imagination and to use it in the way he assumed you would.

Think of Jesus's parables. Many of them are unfinished. Did the elder brother go into the party or did he remain outside in the courtyard complaining and bitter? Did the lost sheep allow itself to be picked up by the shepherd or did it remain cowering in the thicket? The only way we shall discover answers to these questions is by doing what Jesus expected us to do – by entering, with our imagination, into the parables and finishing the story for ourselves.

Think about other aspects of Jesus's teaching – for example, I am the vine, you are the branches, I am the Good

Shepherd. Jesus's listeners had no commentaries to refer to, only the visual aids in front of them: an actual vine, and a real good shepherd. Jesus expected them to visualise the image he was describing as he described it. This is a Middle Eastern way of teaching and Christians in the Middle East today respond to it well. So ask God to deliver you from Western sophistication and the temptation to exalt the mind over the imagination. Ask for the grace to come to him in the way he wants, as a little child, with every part of your being: mind and emotions, will and imagination poised, ready to respond to him. If you find this difficult, tell him some of the reasons.

Re-read John's account of the events of that first Easter Sunday evening. Picture the scene. If you can, step into the Upper Room. Watch Jesus enter the room. Listen to what he says. Feel him breathe his Spirit into you. Write down what you see and sense and feel and hear. Write down, too, your response to him:

11

In joy

Reading: John 15:9–11

As the Father has loved me, so have I loved you. Now remain in my love. If you obey my commands, you will remain in my love, just as I have obeyed my Father's commands and remain in his love. I have told you this so that my joy may be in you and that your joy may be complete. My command is this: Love each other as I have loved you.

It is December – the time when I write the annual newsletter for our friends. And as I look back over the year and try to decide what to write, I am aware that these last twelve months have been crammed with special joy, not because there has been an absence of pain, but because true joy – the kind which comes from sorrows overcome – has dotted my path in the same way as shy primroses dot the hedgerows in spring.

I think, for example, of the occasion when my husband and I were enjoying Cantonese cooking in a Chinese restaurant in China Town in Brisbane, Australia. 'This makes me homesick for Singapore,' I admitted as we ate. Almost before the words had left my lips, I noticed a man smiling at me through the restaurant window. I could scarcely believe my eyes. He was a Singaporean; a friend who, on one of my visits to his country, had begged me to pray for him because he and his wife had been told they were infertile and they both longed for a child.

I did pray. A few months later his wife had written to share their good news: she was pregnant. When the baby was born they sent me a photograph of her which still smiles at me from my prayer-corner wall. And now, here they were, grinning from ear to ear and walking through the restaurant door to greet us. As they placed their miracle baby into my arms, it was as though I was handling joy in a physical form. It was a moment of intense and pure joy.

Later that evening, as we talked to these friends in our hotel room, this joy spilled over into heartfelt thanksgiving to God that he had allowed our paths to cross so mysteriously; that we had all 'happened' to be in the same restaurant in the same town at the same time. I gave thanks, too, for the fulfilment of Jesus's promise: 'My joy shall be in you and your joy shall be full.'

But joy has also come in less tangible forms. It came in Malaysia one summer when my husband and I enjoyed a reunion with ex-members of our congregation who have now returned to their native land. One of the first people to greet me was a girl I had tried to help when she was a student in Nottingham. She reminded me of the dark days of depression she encountered and of the talks we used to have. As I read the gratitude in her eyes, saw the smile of thanks on her lips and felt the warmth of her embrace, I found myself receiving and internalising, not only her love and gratitude, but also the joy which seemed to bubble from her. It was another wonderfully joyful moment.

But perhaps the most moving of them all came in the context of a Communion Service in a sleepy village in England. The service was being conducted by a pastor who, when he nose-dived into the dark tunnel of depression, had given my husband and me the privilege of staying alongside him in the seemingly interminable darkness. But depression had not blunted this man's effectiveness for Christ. The desert experience had produced abundant growth.

And as I watched him press his thumbs into the brown loaf which was to become for us the bread of heaven, into my mind flooded memories of the times I had watched those thumbs being twiddled aimlessly as they expressed the lifelessness that dogged him. And as I watched in wonder as worship lit up his face, I recalled the many occasions when that face had been overshadowed by loneliness and anguish. As I listened to the quiver of excitement in his voice as he confessed: 'I'm so excited by God's Word,' I thought of the hours I had heard that voice bemoan the seeming absence of God and the inability to concentrate on his revealed Word. And I realised that a miracle was unfolding before my eyes.

The miracle was not that this man had experienced a dramatic healing in the sense that one day he was suffering from depression and the next he was enjoying freedom from darkness. His had been a gradual change. God had used a variety of therapies to bring him through the dark valley and into this oasis. But just as I had been given the privilege of staying alongside him in the shadowlands, so now I was being given the even greater privilege and joy of being on the receiving end of his ministry.

'The greater privilege and *joy*.' Yes. It was a moment pregnant with profound joy. Not the shallow, transitory, effervescent kind which, like a will o' the wisp, is here one second and disappears the next, but the deep-down, lasting kind which you savour and ponder and which prompts you to fall on your face at the foot of Christ's cross in wonder, love, adoration and praise; the kind which brings tears to your eyes – tears of *joy*.

That day the God of surprises surprised me by joy. Through the transparency of this humble pastor's ministry, he had shown me what he has been re-creating in the inner recesses of my being: a deep vein of joy. 'My gift to you through others,' he seemed to whisper. 'As you've struggled to absorb their pain so now be enriched by their joy also.'[1]

Reflection

From the verses quoted at the beginning of this section, what do you understand Jesus to be implying? What is the secret of real, deep-down joy?

The Greek word which is translated 'joy' means 'calm delight'. Look back over your life and recall some of the moments of calm delight you have enjoyed. Relive them. Enjoy them all over again. Thank God for them in a written or verbal prayer:

Someone has claimed that 'joy is slow to stir in us', that true joy is attained only gradually. Though Jesus made us depositories of his joy, though Christianity is a religion of joy and though God has filled his world with joy, Christian people have not yet learned to cherish this priceless gift. Would you say that that describes you? If so, ask God to show you why you find it so difficult to make your entry into joy. Make a note of anything he seems to show you:

Jesus shows us how to receive joy. It starts with prayer. 'Ask and you will receive, and your joy will be complete' (John 16:24). Say or write a prayer asking God to give you the gift of joy:

12

In pain

Reading: Isaiah 66:11, 12 JB
*Oh, that you may suck fully
of the milk of her comfort,
That you may nurse with delight
at her abundant breasts.
As nurslings, you shall be carried in her arms
and fondled in her lap;
As a mother comforts her [child]
so will I comfort you.*

'Picture God as a comforting mother holding your inner child close to her breasts,' suggested the author of the book I was using to help me in my meditation. When I read that suggestion my first reaction was to recoil. Then I felt my heart freeze. Something inside me refused to continue meditating. I closed the book, put it down and, with a mighty heave, pushed away the ambivalence which had risen unbidden to the surface of my mind. I was overseas on a teaching tour at the time and faced a busy day, so I spent the rest of my prayer time preparing myself for the day ahead and thought no more about this curious act of avoidance.

Two days later, however, while I was still 'coming to' as it were after a good night's sleep, it was as though the bedroom where I was staying was filled with the presence of God. It almost seemed as though the Beloved had come through the open window and enfolded me in tenderness. In fact, when I tried to explain it later to the person in whose home I was staying, I simply said: 'I had a visit from the Tender One this morning,' and I remember being relieved when she asked no questions but seemed to know what I meant.

I did not know that morning what I now know: that God was preparing to take me on another lap of the journey into wholeness. That morning, I simply luxuriated in the tender, gentle, motherly love which enfolded me.

Over the next few days, while I stayed in that home, every morning started in the same way: with the acute awareness of the enveloping presence of the Tender One. This continued for several days after I had left that place which had become holy ground for me. In the retreat house where I was leading an Easter retreat, I was still conscious of the overshadowing of the Tender One.

But then everything changed. For no apparent reason, I found myself reliving, in my dreams and in my prayer times, the trauma of my birth. I was still on the teaching tour, still busy, still coping outwardly; but inwardly, I was in turmoil. At first, I thought the Tender One had deserted me but one warm, sunny day, as I sat on the shore of a lake trying to understand the inner turmoil and trying to spread it before God, the loving presence was there for me again – me the adult and me the baby. As memories of my birth flooded my memory yet again, I felt tender arms receiving me into the world and instinctively I knew that a deep, inner wound had been touched.

At first I failed to appreciate the connection between the visit of the Tender One and the exposure of this primal pain but during the retreat which sandwiched these two

events, I 'happened' to discover a little book on the
bookshelves of the retreat house: *The Way of Tenderness*
by Kevin O'Shea. In it, he explains that tenderness

> *is not something efficient, executive, managerial. It does
> not belong to the domain of getting things done. There
> is nothing violent in it, nothing strong in it. It is not
> manipulative, not task-oriented, not a thing of action.
> It belongs to being, rather than to doing, and to feeling,
> and resting, in peace, at depth. It is a quality of being
> related, it is the limitlessness of being so, without strain
> or fear. There is something of love in it. It is the
> relaxedness that comes from knowing by experience
> that one is thoroughly and totally loved . . . If we
> could ask ourselves, 'at this very moment, right here,
> do I honestly believe that God likes me – not loves me,
> since He has to do that theologically, but likes me?' And
> if we could say, 'Yes He does,' and mean it, there would
> be a relaxedness and a gentleness with us that is close to
> what we are calling 'tenderness' . . . We could feel that we
> could love our whole life-story, that we are graced, and
> made beautiful, by the providence of our own history.
> That is what 'tenderness' might mean.[1]*

The phrase, 'knowing by experience that one is thoroughly
and totally loved', and the sentence, 'We could feel that we
could love our whole life-story', seemed to sum up what I
was experiencing, in greater depth than ever before.

In the climate in which we live, when scores of books
have been written about counselling, inner healing and
prayer ministry, it seems timely to underline that God's
healing can and frequently does come in the quiet, undra-
matic moments when he encircles us with love – as we
walk, as we work, as we contemplate the wonders of
creation or as we meditate on the scriptures. It happens
not infrequently, for example, that we can be reading a
familiar gospel story or a passage like the one from Isaiah
which I was reading that morning in my friend's house,

when, if we are tuned in to our innermost self, we will detect an inner reaction or some strong feelings. If we listen to those emotions, moods and responses, they can point us to the need for inner healing.[2]

Reflection

Re-read those verses from Isaiah where God likens himself to a good, nurturing mother. What kind of reaction does that produce in you? Tell God about it:

Recall occasions when God has come to you with tenderness and compassion. What kind of response do these memories prompt in you?

Do you believe God *likes* you? If you're not sure, ask him.
Record his response if you sense he gives you one. Maybe
a verse of scripture will come into your head, or perhaps
a line from a hymn or a chorus, or a picture or some words
which God seems to whisper:

Draw a picture or diagram which sums up the way you
see yourself in relationship to God. Draw a second picture
or diagram which sums up the way you would wish your
relationship with God to become:

13

When bereaved

Reading: Ruth 1:3–19

Now Elimelech, Naomi's husband, died, and she was left with her two sons. They married Moabite women, one named Orpah and the other Ruth. After they had lived [in Moab] for about ten years, both Mahlon and Kilion also died, and Naomi was left without her two sons and her husband.

When she heard in Moab that the Lord had come to the aid of his people by providing food for them, Naomi and her daughters-in-law prepared to return home . . . Then Naomi said to her two daughters-in-law, 'Go back, each of you, to your mother's home. May the Lord show kindness to you, as you have shown to your dead and to me. May the Lord grant that each of you will find rest in the home of another husband.'

Then she kissed them and they wept aloud . . . Then Orpah kissed her mother-in-law good-bye, but Ruth clung to her:

'Don't urge me to leave you or to turn back from you. Where you go I will go, and where you stay I will stay. Your people will be my people and your God my God. Where you die I will die, and there I will be buried. May the Lord deal with me, be it ever so severely, if anything but death separates you and me.' . . . So the two women went on until they came to Bethlehem.

As so often happens, even though my mother had been ill for many years the end came suddenly. When my father and I were disgorged from the funeral car at the top of the stony church drive, we were ushered to our place behind the waiting coffin. The sight of that elm box with its brass handles made me reel. The last time we had stood together on that spot was on my wedding day when my father was so proud to have me on his arm, dressed in all my wedding finery. Now we were dressed soberly and together we were giving my mother away. We could no longer deny the harsh reality: Mum was dead. For a few agonising minutes the anaesthetic of grief wore off. Our wounds were exposed. And we stumbled, weeping, behind that flower-studded box into the church. But once we reached the church porch everything changed. 'Look at all those people,' my father whispered. I looked – and gasped. The church was packed. The presence of those people who had taken the trouble to take time off work to come to say goodbye to my mother strengthened us more than anything else could have done in that moment. I saw my godfather . . . I noticed Mrs Fursman who had been a waitress with my mother . . . and I spotted several neighbours.

The strength that flowed into me as I stared at them, emptily but gratefully, took me by surprise. I did not know in those days what I now know: that the word comfort means to strengthen. What I did know was that these people who were not saying or doing anything except by being there were giving me untold comfort.

And so were the words of scripture. As we processed up the aisle, those words of Jesus which the vicar was reading aloud tumbled round my bruised heart and soothed the pain: 'Jesus said: "I am the resurrection and the life. He who believes in me will live, even though he dies; and whoever lives and believes in me will never die."' (John 11:25–6). 'It's not your mother in that box,' these words seemed to say. 'That's only her earthly remains. She lives on.' I knew that to be true and again I was strengthened – so much so that I could sing the hymns with conviction and confidence. God's presence and love seemed very real. And had not my father and I read together on the night my mother died those wonderful promises penned by the Psalmist:

> *He who dwells in the shelter of the Most High*
> *will rest in the shadow of the Almighty . . .*
> *He will cover you with his feathers,*
> *and under his wings you will find refuge.*
>
> *(Psalm 91:1,4)*

Even so I was grateful for others who incarnated God's love for my father and me. My eighty-year-old Uncle Bob did this in the funeral car as we travelled to the crematorium. He spent the entire journey quizzing me about my relationship with God.

'I was watching you during the service,' he said. 'You seemed to believe everything you were hearing and seeing. I wish I could find such assurance of God's love.

'It's strange,' he went on. 'I've been playing the double bass in Handel's *Messiah* every year for as long as I care to remember. I've listened to all those wonderful words. But I still lack the trust in God which seems to be your mainstay.'

In reply I was able to testify to the fact that I was experiencing the divine overshadowing the Psalmist describes and that it was under the wings of God that I found my security in times of testing and trauma. He listened. And giving voice to God's faithfulness increased that sense in me of the peace of God which defies understanding and circumstances, and pervades even in the middle of the storm.[1]

Reflection

Often the dying person's relatives and friends suffer more than the dying person. Diminished consciousness in the sick person has an anaesthetising effect which is not felt by those who watch. They see only the dying person's changing appearance and increasing weakness. They may even tune in to their emotional turmoil and fear. Even when the patient has reached the point of accepting death those who stand by are brought face to face with the real sting of the grave – separation. So pray, today, for thousands of refugees all over the world who have been forced to watch their loved ones die. And cut out of a newspaper or magazine photographs of the bereaved to help you to remember to pray for grief-stricken people all over the world. You might like to stick it here.

The work of grief cannot be hurried even for the believer. And every bereaved person needs several Ruths to help them cope with the many adjustments that need to be made when a loved one dies. Ruth supported Naomi in a whole variety of ways. She refused to abandon her mother-in-law and stayed right alongside her until she could re-negotiate life on a new set of terms, without her husband and sons. She listened to Naomi's bitterness and anger without reproaching her. And Ruth gave generous practical help – like working through the heat of the day to ensure that there was food for both of them to eat. Ask God to show you if there is a bereaved person you could help – by listening to them talk about the one they have lost, by looking with them at photographs of the loved one, by asking them about the funeral, by cooking a casserole or by providing a shoulder to cry on.

If you have been bereaved yourself, write down the names of the people who were Ruths to you. Then write a prayer thanking God for them. If you have never been through the pain of bereavement, tell God how you feel about staying alongside others in their pain. Ask him to give you a sensitivity to the bereaved which fleshes out his care and concern:

14

In times of loss

Reading: Psalm 31:9–12, 14

Be merciful to me, O Lord, for I am in distress;
my eyes grow weak with sorrow,
my soul and my body with grief.
My life is consumed by anguish
and my years by groaning;
my strength fails because of my affliction,
and my bones grow weak . . .
I am forgotten . . . as though I were dead;
I have become like broken pottery . . .

But I trust in you, O Lord;
I say, 'You are my God.'
My times are in your hands . . .
Let your face shine on your servant;
save me in your unfailing love.

A student nurse who knew she was dying wrote to her colleagues in an attempt to help them to understand how they could best help her:

Please believe me, if you care, you can't go wrong. Just admit that you care. That is really what we are searching for. We may ask for whys and wherefores, but we don't really expect answers. Don't run away – wait – all I want to know is that there will be someone to hold my hand when I need it. I am afraid. Death . . . is new to me. I've never died before.[1]

Life's little deaths

When we use the word 'death' we almost always mean the loss of life. Yet death is only one extreme example of loss. Life challenges us to undergo all kinds of other losses – the loss of a limb through accident or amputation, the loss of a child through a miscarriage, the loss of a job through redundancy, the loss of hope through the inability to conceive a child, the loss of parts of the body through disfigurement or surgery: mastectomy, hysterectomy; the loss of someone special when a boy-girlfriend relationship terminates, or when a close friend moves, the unlikelihood of finding a life-partner, the break-up of a marriage, the closing of the chapter which retirement brings. Looked at in this way, we are surrounded by people who are suffering the trauma of mini-deaths and we shall experience many of them ourselves.

What happens in life's little losses is exactly the same process people suffer when a loved one dies. At first you feel stunned: you can't take it in. You look at life as though you were looking through double-glazed windows or from an aeroplane. You are aware that it is happening but, although life goes on as normal, it seems to bear little relevance to you. This is the stage when your feelings are deep-frozen; when you can stare at a beautiful view yet not see it, when a blackbird can be singing in the trees outside your window, but you are incapable of hearing it. It is the phase when any form of beauty passes you by.

These feelings eventually thaw out. The tears might then flow fast and freely; it is important that you allow them to do so. They are a language. They are expressing feelings so deep that they cannot be summed up in words. Even if you are a man, weep; to cry is not unmanly or un-Christlike: 'Jesus wept' (John 11:35).

'Grief-work', as this process is called by psychologists, almost always includes not only tears, but anger: we find someone to blame. Then there's the pining and the searching. When a loved one dies, this can be agonising because, however hard you search, the loved one cannot be found. But when an ex-boyfriend or girlfriend is only a telephone call away, the temptation is to pick up the phone and to make contact. That is why a couple whose relationship is dying will often drive their friends crazy. One day the relationship is off, the following weekend it is on again. This yo-yo relationship might continue, up and down, up and down for weeks, even months, before it finally fizzles out.

These painful grief procedures must be worked through; the pain must not be repressed. Repress it and it will pop up again in a disguised form a few months later. Work through it, like a tug-boat plodding its way upstream, and you will find a miracle taking place however slowly and gradually. You will nose your way into unexplored and exhilarating freedoms; you can have a new and deep relationship with Christ.

This, at least, was my experience on one occasion. When I was an undergraduate, I fell in love with a fellow member of the committee of the Christian Union. He was the president, I was the secretary. For months I loved from afar. Then I plucked up courage to allow my feelings to be known. Our relationship deepened as the months passed. But when, one cold November day, he told me that 'it was not God's will' for us to go out together, I was devastated.

I remember studying the Song of Solomon at that time and being stirred by God's bridegroom-love. I remember his gentle in-breathing, his tender touching of those grazed and bruised places deep within. Although that crisis erupted nearly forty years ago, I look back on it as one of the lasting landmarks of my spiritual growth.

In my lostness, God found me. And to be found by him
is special.[2]

Reflection

The Psalmist paints a poignant picture of himself in Psalm
31:12: 'I have become like broken pottery.' What does that
pen-picture communicate to you?

Think of occasions when you have suffered one or more of
life's little deaths. What picture would you use to describe
yourself at that time? It might help you to try to draw it.

Who or what helped you work through the pain? Thank
God for these helps along the way.

Pray today for any known to you who are dying or struggling to come to terms with life's little deaths. Try to stay alongside them lovingly and sensitively. Or if you, yourself, are in pain, follow the Psalmist's example (v.14, 15). Let the experience give birth to a prayer – of complaint, of anguish, of trust – or a mixture of all three together with other emotions:

15

When depressed

Reading: 1 Kings 19:3–9

Elijah was afraid and ran for his life. When he came to Beersheba in Judah, he left his servant there, while he himself went a day's journey into the desert. He came to a broom tree, sat down under it and prayed that he might die. 'I have had enough, Lord,' he said. 'Take my life; I am no better than my ancestors.' Then he lay down under the tree and fell asleep.

All at once an angel touched him and said, 'Get up and eat.' He looked around, and there by his head was a cake of bread baked over hot coals, and a jar of water. He ate and drank and then lay down again.

The angel of the Lord came back a second time and touched him and said, 'Get up and eat, for the journey is too much for you.' So he got up and ate and drank. Strengthened by that food, he travelled for forty days and forty nights until he reached Horeb, the mountain of God. There he went into a cave and spent the night.

Christian and depressed?

It is perfectly possible to be a committed Christian *and* to suffer from depression. Having a firm faith in God is no insurance policy against this dis-ease of the emotions nor even an inoculation against it. Many great men and women of God have been entrusted with this mysterious sickness of the soul. In addition to Elijah, there was the Psalmist. He sums up the feelings and experiences of the depressed person so succinctly that, when we are depressed, many of us turn instinctively to certain Psalms: 'My tears have been my food day and night . . .' (Psalms 42:3).

Then there was J. B. Phillips. Unable to shake off the symptoms of depression, he was forced to resign from his first living and go into hiding in Swanage where he corresponded with other depressives. Leslie Weatherhead was one. In a letter, this great preacher who used to thrill huge congregations each Sunday with his preaching confesses to: 'over two hundred hours of "analysis" thirty years ago. I finally emerged, but it took years . . .'.[1] And there was William Cowper, so becalmed by depression that when offered a responsible post in the House of Lords, he succumbed to an anxiety state and was so agitated that he tried several times to kill himself.

I learned that many of the world's geniuses had suffered similarly: Isaac Newton, Beethoven, Darwin, Van Gogh, Tolstoy, Spurgeon and Martin Luther. Their inner turmoil did not block their creativity. On the contrary, their suffering seemed to contribute to their greatness. While J. B. Phillips was depressed he translated the whole of the New Testament into a powerful paraphrase. While William Cowper was depressed he wrote some of his best hymns and poems. And while C. H. Spurgeon was depressed he preached some of his finest sermons.

This taught me that I must not waste suffering. Instead I must learn to use it. Even so this did nothing to alleviate the pain when I nose-dived into the tunnel of depression once more. The feelings were always the same – or at least a variation on a miserable theme.

My mind was be-fogged, confused. To think became too much of an effort. My energy level seemed to have ebbed away. In its place a debilitating lethargy would sweep over the shore of my life and refuse to go away. Because my mind seemed so sluggish, the quick actions and reactions of others felt like a kick in the stomach. Cruel. Insensitive. Unloving. Laughter jarred. Singing grated on the exhausted nerves. And because everything seemed so grim, the slightest disappointment seemed capable of knocking me off balance and plunging me into a deeper despair. Even the sun failed to cheer me. 'The sun is shining but everything is dark – very dark,' I wrote in my journal. And the phrase 'everything hurts' seemed like a punctuation mark in this same journal.

I was one of the fortunate ones. Mine was a recurrent depression, not a psychotic one. During the short intermissions I could think rationally, read, pray and sense the presence of God. And I was fortunate enough to see a purpose in what was happening to me, at least some of time. In one of the early remissions, I remember reeling from the shock of what I was going through and talking to God about it. Two passages of scripture and a particular word of comfort reassured and strengthened me at this time. First God seemed to remind me that soon after his anointing by the Spirit at his baptism, Jesus was driven into the wilderness where he was tested. This testing, I discovered, was not designed to break the Son of God but rather to strengthen him for the ministry that lay ahead, in the same way as metal must be tested before it is usable. In my most rational moments, and even when I was crawling through the endlessly long and dark tunnel of depression, I remembered this and clung on to the hope that maybe this was what was happening to me.

The second scripture came in the form of a promise from Jesus, which again I clung to when the going was tough. 'Simon, Simon,' Jesus had said to his beloved disciple,

'Satan has asked to sift you as wheat. But I have prayed for you' (Luke 22: 31–2). Those words 'I have prayed for you' brought such comfort that I wrote on a piece of paper, **'Jesus is praying for me now'**, and stuck it on the wall of my prayer room so that I would be reminded of God's holding hand even when I could no longer feel or experience it.

And the comforting words which I sensed God whispered were these:

> *Just as nature is about to be stripped bare, the petals will fall from the roses, the leaves will flutter from the trees and the earth will lie hard and bare, so I will strip you. You will lie exposed, naked, in all your vulnerability. But . . . this is not the stripping of vindictiveness or revenge; it is the stripping of great love. With the nakedness of your winter comes my promise that just as the springtime will bring the re-clothing of nature in all its freshness, newness and vitality, so your clothing will be accomplished by me. Your new garments will exceed, in beauty and usefulness, anything you have previously experienced . . .[2]*

Reflection

Elijah's depression was almost certainly caused by exhaustion or what is commonly known as burn-out today. He had exhausted himself in winning great victories for God. Exhaustion can distort our perception. This happened to Elijah; and he collapsed. Notice how God comes to him – not with a rebuke, nor with a complaint but with simple, practical, healing gifts: of food and sleep. Tell God how you feel about this practical, sensitive demonstration of love:

Reflect on occasions when you have similarly suffered
from burn-out or depression, discouragement or disappointment. Recall the ways in which God has revealed his
love to you. Thank him in a verbal or a written prayer:

Pray for any, particularly pastors or missionaries, who are
becalmed by depression today. Ask God to show you
whether you can help in any way: with a letter, with
encouragement or by giving some practical help.

16

When lonely

Reading: Isaiah 46:3–4

Listen to me . . .
you whom I have upheld since you were conceived,
and have carried since your birth.
Even to your old age and grey hairs
I am he, I am he who will sustain you.
I have made you and I will carry you.
I will sustain you and I will rescue you.

Loneliness: full of potential beauty

Loneliness is a feeling: or, more accurately, a jumble of feelings. It is the feeling that you matter to people, not for who you are, but for what you can do. For some, it goes deeper than that: it is the anxiety that you do not matter at all. If you died tomorrow, no one would even notice, let alone care. It is a feeling of alienation . . . a feeling of being cut off by others. It is a feeling that no one is even aware of your heart-hunger, *your* need for care, love and support . . . the feeling that you have ceased to be important to a particular person or body of people. Loneliness attacks the senses so that you feel isolated from your peers. You seem to be rejected, estranged, abandoned; you believe that nowhere are you fully understood.

Most people spend much of their lives avoiding listening to the language of this very basic human loneliness which is common to single people and married people alike. In hospital we cannot do that. There, all our escape routes are blocked: we have no meetings to attend, no sermons to prepare, no stream of urgent telephone calls to make or receive; instead we have plenty of that elusive commodity we call time. And in the long, sometimes sleepless hours of the night as well as in the uninterrupted moments of the day, while we are alone with our thoughts, our loneliness stares us in the face and either leers or smiles at us . . .

In hospital, visiting times more than any other time can trigger off such loneliness. That, at least, was my experience. So much so that in my journal I described visiting time as a 'bitter-sweet occasion': 'Again, it's visiting time and I'm poised between trying to be patient, accepting, recognising that nobody may come and yet so much hoping for at least one visitor.'

On this occasion, my loneliness was not alleviated by the appearance of a person. Something much more significant happened. It was as though I was given the courage so to listen to the language of my inner longings that, instead of running from my apparent emptiness, I could face it and even make a descent into the eerie chasm. As I did so, a miracle seemed to take place. I realised that loneliness is a mirage. Deep within myself is not emptiness but fullness: the presence of the indwelling Holy Trinity – Father, Son and Holy Spirit. Whereas I had been pining for people, God was wanting to draw me into a deeper intimacy than any person could give: the intimacy of the love which flows so freely between the three members of the Godhead.

As I made my descent, I found myself drawn into that circle of love where I felt held in an almost tangible, overpowering peace; overwhelmed with the realisation that I was being enfolded in a love which was more pure, more kind, more caring, more tender than the deepest of human love. Was it a coincidence that the following day I stumbled upon the following in Jean Vanier's little book, *Treasures of the Heart?* I think not.

> *Even the most beautiful community can never heal the wound of loneliness that we carry . . . It is only when we discover that this loneliness can become sacrament that we touch wisdom, for this sacrament is purification and presence of God. If we stop fleeing from the solitude, and if we accept our wound, we will discover that this is the way to meet Jesus Christ. It is when we stop fleeing into work and activity, noise and illusion, when we remain conscious of our wound, that we will meet God. He is the Paraclete, the One who responds to our cry, which comes from the darkness of our loneliness . . .*[1]

Loneliness, I discovered that day, need not be a blight to the soul. Loneliness is full of potential beauty. If we will explore its nooks and crannies and work in them rather than running from them, loneliness can become the place where God's whisper is heard and his presence most keenly felt.[2]

Reflection

Billy Graham once claimed that loneliness is the greatest problem facing mankind today. Mother Teresa of Calcutta once made the staggering claim that it is easier to relieve material poverty than to alleviate this poverty of the soul. No one can take out an insurance policy against this heart-hunger which gnaws at our innermost being from time to time. It sometimes seems as though successful people are more susceptible to loneliness than others. So

Albert Einstein once wrote: 'It is strange to be known so universally and yet to be so lonely,' while the actress Joan Crawford ended her own life: 'lonely, bitter, reclusive'. So ask yourself, 'What do I do when I am lonely?':

Re-read the verses from Isaiah. Although they were first addressed to Israel as a nation, they may also be absorbed by us today. So place your own name in the space at the end of the first line. You might even like to copy out those verses and include your own name as you do so:

Trace the times when, since your birth, you have been conscious of God's support and love. Let these memories give you the courage to explore the nooks and crannies of your loneliness when it sweeps over you.

Pray for any who are lonely at this moment: missionaries working overseas, refugees who have left or lost loved ones, homes and possessions, those who are lonely because they are suffering from burn-out. Find a picture of one such person and let it prompt you to pray regularly for the world's lonely ones.

17

When needing forgiveness

Reading: John 19:16b, 17, 28–30

The soldiers took charge of Jesus. Carrying his own cross, he went out to the place of the Skull (which in Aramaic is called Golgotha). Here they crucified him, and with him two others – one on each side and Jesus in the middle . . .

Later . . . Jesus said, 'I am thirsty.' A jar of wine vinegar was there, so they soaked a sponge in it, put the sponge on a stalk of the hyssop plant, and lifted it to Jesus' lips. When he had received the drink, Jesus said, 'It is finished.' With that, he bowed his head and gave up his spirit.

The freedom God gives us from the penalty of sin is awesome: it is mystery. But equally awesome and mysterious are those words Jesus uttered from the cross: 'It is finished.' These words made a powerful impact on me on one occasion. I was gazing at a crude wooden cross which someone had erected in the mountains where I was leading a retreat. As I gazed at the two pieces of wood which had been lashed together by a piece of rope and mounted on a pile of rocks, I spread before God a particular failure I wanted to leave with him. As I expressed my longing to be set free a triumphant roar seemed to come from the cross and echo round the mountain range: 'It is finished!' I was startled by the uncanny power with which those words seemed laced. 'What are you trying to say to me, Lord?' I asked.

The same words reached me with even greater force: 'It is finished!' And I wanted to weep because, suddenly, I knew what those words meant. My failure and I no longer belonged to one another. Jesus, by dying on a crude cross, had separated us. A severance had taken place, setting me free to be me once more. There would be no need to mention this failure to God again. Love for Jesus welled up in my heart reminding me of his claim that those who have been forgiven much, love much.

Because the love within me was so strong, I asked the Beloved to show me how he had felt as he hung nailed to the cross and I tried, as it were, to step into his skin as he hung there. Whereupon a surge of joy filled me. I sensed I understood why the prayer of the penitent thief: 'Jesus, remember me when you come into your Kingdom,' had elicited from Jesus a response of joy, strength and relief: 'Today you will be with me in Paradise.' Even though his body was being tortured, it gave Jesus joy to see that his agony was not in vain. One man, at least, was availing himself of the freedom for which Jesus was paying such a phenomenal price.

Jesus could reassure the penitent because the word 'finished' is a legal word meaning 'accomplished'. It was often scrawled across bills in New Testament times. It means 'Paid!', 'Transaction completed', 'Score settled!'

Like the thieves hanging each side of Jesus, we have all offended our holy God in a whole variety of ways – not least by spurning his overtures of love and by refusing to allow God to be God. This is the essence of sin and, as Paul reminds us, 'the wages of sin is death' (Romans 6:23). But just as Jesus rescued the penitent, so he continues to rescue those who repent. Because Jesus died on the cross and rose again, we have been set free from the punishment that should have been ours: our debt has been cancelled, paid. We are free from sin's penalty: God has forgiven us.

When God forgives, he does not play a game of 'Let's pretend': 'Let's pretend they never sinned.' No. He sees us as we are: soiled, helpless, innately sinful. He knows what he is taking on when he promises to love us. Even so, he applies the righteousness of Jesus to us. When he looks on us he sees, not the stain of the sin which has penetrated every particle of our being, but his pure and holy Son. It is as though we have been clothed in Jesus's own spotless, unsoiled garment. This is deep mystery: it can never be fully understood or fully explained – only contemplated with hearts bowed in adoration, love and praise as we recall that the freedom it bestows is instant. Irreversible. Complete. The penalty has been paid. God will not go back on this act. The deed is done.[1]

Reflection
Read the following invitation from God:

My child, let it be your privilege, each day, to dwell upon my sacrifice, made for the whole world. In my suffering love upon the cross you see a continuing process . . . the unrequited love which pursues my children – yearning for the slightest response, and profoundly grateful when one of those children surrenders his or her life to me. On the cross, you see my heart of love crushed, for the moment, by the force of evil which darkens this universe. Then you see the bursting forth again of love's power . . . in my Father's victory

. . . Here, at the cross, give me your heart, anew, every day.

Now, gaze at a cross or a picture of one. Ask yourself the following four questions:

1. What is God saying through this cross?

2. What is God saying *to me* through this cross?

3. If I could step into the skin of the Saviour who died on that cross, how might I feel about the world, the penitent thief, the by-standers, and myself?

4. Write or say a prayer that sums up your response – or respond by drawing a picture or by writing a poem:

18

When angry

Readings: Ephesians 4:25–7; Proverbs 21:14

*Each of you must put off falsehood and speak truthfully
to his neighbour, for we are all members of one body. 'In
your anger do not sin.' Do not let the sun go down while
you are still angry, and do not give the devil a foothold.*

A gift given in secret soothes anger.

One minute David and I were sauntering along in the
warm sunshine, hand in hand, contented companions.
The next minute pain prised us apart. One minute we
were as one as we stood drinking in the grandeur of the
scenery: blue sky, snow-crowned mountains, pink and
white almond blossom, pillar-straight pines. The next
minute it was as though a chill cloud blanketed this world.
Yet there was not a cloud in sight. Only the silent hostility
between us spoiled the splendour of the day.

It was hot. David, my husband, wilts in warm weather.
We wandered into a supermarket.

'Look! Ice-cold drinks in the fridge! I'm going to
buy some.'

'But they're all *fizzy* drinks. You know I don't like fizzy stuff. Let's go on a bit. There's a café on top of that hill out there. I can smell the coffee. We could sit in the sun, have a drink, and rest.'

'Coffee! Who wants coffee in this weather? Cold drinks are much better. Come on, let's buy some.'

I watched David choose a can of cool Coke from the fridge, swallowed my anger, and walked out of the supermarket in front of him. I was seething inwardly at this demonstration of seeming selfishness on his part. Couldn't he see that I had needs too? Why, when we're abroad, does he always insist on having all the money so that I couldn't even go off and buy a cup of coffee on my own? Why doesn't he listen when I state a preference?

'D'you want a sip of my Coke? It's very nice.'

David's teasing burst in on this silent stream of resentment. To his amazement I burst into tears, leaving him wondering why my mood had swung so swiftly from contentment to utter dejection.

'Is everything all right? Have I done something wrong?'

By this time the emotions rising inside me were so strong, I dared not speak. I stood silent, sullen, sorrowful, gazing at the mountains and almond blossom whose still splendour now seemed to mock me. Detached from David, I was detached from this magnificence also. All I wanted was a hole where I could take the ugliness of my emotions, empty them out and hide until some sort of equilibrium could be established between us again. But we were overseas: I knew of nowhere to hide. So we drove, in snow-cold silence, back to our apartment, victims of conflict.[1]

The question I used to ask in those days was: 'Lord, when are you going to change my husband so that our marriage can be more harmonious?' But as I learned to work through anger and resentment with God, the Holy Spirit seemed to put a new question on my lips and in my heart: 'Lord, how do you want *me* to change so that our marriage can be more harmonious?'

God, I found, never failed to answer that question.

One way he answered it was by showing me what anger is and what it is not. The first thing he showed me was that anger, of itself, is not a sin. If it was a sin, neither the Psalmist nor Paul would have said, 'Be angry but do not sin.' If anger, of itself, was a sin, Jesus would not have been angry because he was the sinless one. Anger is a neutral emotion which may or may not become sinful depending on what we do with it. Anger is energy. This energy can be channelled for good or for evil; it can be used creatively, or destructively to hurt people.

I also discovered that anger is a secondary emotion. Lurking beneath rage, there is always another emotion. We therefore need to discern the nature and the cause of this primary emotion. When we probe, we will almost always find that inside the angry person cowers a hurting, rejected or frightened little figure – a part of ourselves God longs to touch.

When I stopped to analyse the quarrel that erupted between my husband and me, ostensibly over a thirst-quenching drink on a hot day in the mountains, I realised that the question of the drink was simply the peg on which we were hanging the frustration of months. We had been overworking; sacrificing our marital relationship on the altar of parish work: counselling, preaching, teaching, writing, befriending. We were well aware that overbusyness was siphoning off vital energy from our relationship: spiritual, sexual, emotional. We were depriving each other of time, attention and the cherishing on which zestful marriages thrive. What was being expressed through that quarrel was the accumulation of months of unresolved tension and unmet needs.

A month later, after we had unwound together on that sabbatical leave, revised the art of relaxing together, studied and prayed together, that quarrel could not have flared up.[2] But the quarrel *did* flare up and, in the quietness of the apartment where we were staying, God came to me in rather the same way as the Good Samaritan came to the man who was mugged on the Jerusalem–Jericho road.

He touched, soothed, cleansed and healed the inner hurts
without which I would not have had the grace to forgive.

Reflection

When they are angry, some people lose their temper,
others leave the room or walk away from the person with
whom they are angry, while others grow very silent. This is
often referred to as the Fight, Flight or Freeze Syndrome.
What do you do when you are angry?

Think of an occasion when you were angry. Remind
yourself of the events which gave rise to the anger. What
was the primary emotion? Hurt, rejection, fear or . . .?
Which of these emotions did you take to God: the anger
or the hurt? And which of the emotions did you share
with your colleagues, your friend or your spouse (if you
are married)?

Ask God to give you the grace to expose the primary emotion to him so that he can come and touch and soothe the hurting you, and give you the strength, when the time is ripe, to forgive. In order to help us tune in to the primary emotion, when we are angry, he will often lovingly whisper: 'Tell me the whole story. Tell me *why* you're hurting.' Do you need to tell him 'the whole story' now?

Chew over Paul's injunction: '*In your anger do not sin*.' What do you think he means by this?

19

When forgiving

Reading: Matthew 18:21–35

Peter came to Jesus and asked, 'Lord, how many times shall I forgive my brother when he sins against me? Up to seven times?'

Jesus answered, 'I tell you, not seven times, but seventy-seven times. Therefore, the kingdom of heaven is like a king who wanted to settle accounts with his servants. As he began the settlement, a man who owed him ten thousand talents was brought to him. Since he was not able to pay, the master ordered that he and his wife and his children and all that he had be sold to repay the debt.

'The servant fell on his knees before him. "Be patient with me," he begged, "and I will pay back everything." The servant's master took pity on him, cancelled the debt and let him go.

'But when that servant went out, he found one of his fellow-servants who owed him a hundred denarii. He grabbed him and began to choke him. "Pay back what you owe me!" he demanded.

'His fellow-servant fell to his knees and begged him, "Be patient with me, and I will pay you back."

'But he refused. Instead, he went off and had the man thrown into prison until he could pay the debt. When the other servants saw what had happened, they were greatly distressed and went and told their master everything that had happened.

'The master called the servant in. "You wicked servant," he said, "I cancelled all that debt of yours because you begged me to. Shouldn't you have had mercy on your fellow-servant just as I had on you?" In anger his master turned him over to the jailers to be tortured, until he should pay back all he owed.

'This is how my heavenly Father will treat each of you unless you forgive your brother from the heart.'

Jesus reminds us on many occasions that our responsibility is not simply to receive his free forgiveness for the failures which blight our lives. In addition to that, in all our relationships with other people, we have a responsibility to extend that free forgiveness to anyone who has failed us in any way. So when Peter asks him the startling question: 'Lord, how many times shall I forgive my brother when he sins against me? Up to seven times?', Jesus replies, 'I tell you, not seven times, but seventy-seven times.' And Jesus goes further when he gives this clear exhortation: 'When you stand praying, if you hold anything against anyone, forgive him, so that your Father in heaven may forgive you your sins' (Mark 11:25).

When married couples are taking this exhortation seriously and obeying this command of Jesus, they are finding that their marriages are being mended by God. Indeed, more marriages are completely mended through the grace of forgiveness than through any other method that I know of.

I think of a couple my husband and I met after one of our Marriage Fulfilment Conferences where we had spoken on the need to forgive. This couple invited us to their home for a meal because they were anxious to tell us their story. They had not intended to come to the seminars which had been organised by their local church, but God seemed to insist that they should come and so they gave away the concert tickets they had bought for that night and attended the meetings.

When they came, their marriage was in deep trouble. The husband was involved in full-time Christian work and his wife helped him as best she could. But she had the home to run and two small children to look after, so time was in short supply. On his own admission her husband was a workaholic. It rarely occurred to him to spend time with the family or take his wife out. He was overtired, his wife was overtired and whenever they were together rows and quarrels would erupt. Their children grew increasingly aware of the friction between their parents and consequently became frighteningly insecure. 'They refused to go to sleep at night,' the wife explained. 'They would wake up crying, wanting to come into Mummy and Daddy's bed. They were frightened that we were going to separate; that if they went to sleep in their own beds they would wake up in the morning and find that one of us had gone for good.'

At the end of the seminar on forgiveness, we gave couples an opportunity to recall habits or attitudes in their partner which they disliked or which had caused them to be hurt or upset, and then we asked a question: 'Will you forgive your partner for that?' In the silence which followed, couples were invited to forgive their partner. Unknown to the other, as they knelt beside one another in church, these two both forgave each other. When the meeting ended, tears were rolling down their cheeks as they asked one another that most healing question: 'Will you forgive me for the way I have failed you and our marriage?' As they responded to that question, they resolved to live differently in the days that lay ahead.

When they returned home, they tried to explain to their children what had happened and told them that Mummy and Daddy would not be quarrelling any more in the way they had been doing for months. The children slept soundly. And while we were there, both children played outside quite happily showing no signs of insecurity. For this family, forgiveness brought healing not simply to the marriage but to the entire family. 'It was worth giving away those concert tickets,' the husband said. 'God had something much better in store for us than good music.'[1]

Reflection

It is not only married people who need to forgive each other. In the imperfection of the world, conflict will erupt in even the most harmonious relationships – between colleagues, friends, parents and children as well as husbands and wives. Ask God to show you today whether there is someone against whom you have been harbouring bitterness or resentment or hatred. Listen to give God an opportunity to shine his torch into a corner of your life you may not have seen.

To forgive means 'to drop', 'to let go'; so to refuse to forgive means to cling. Forgiveness therefore faces us with a choice: to let go of bitterness, hatred and resentment or to cling to it. If God has shown you someone you need to forgive, you are now faced with a choice: to let go of your negativity or to hang on to it. Which will you choose? If you find it difficult to let go, tell God why it is so hard.

To forgive does not mean to forget. It starts by remembering, as vividly as possible, the reasons why you became embittered in the first place. When we recall the incident and the hurt which was inflicted, we become aware of the pain which God wants to touch and heal. If you are aware of such hidden, secret pain, begin to spread it before God now. Ask him to anoint it with the healing balm of his love. This healing work cannot be hurried so be as patient with yourself as God is.

If you are finding it impossible to let go of negative emotions, clench your fist around a stone or cling to a chair or table. Notice how unfree this act of clinging makes you. Recognise that you are as unfree emotionally as that. If you feel you can, ask God for the grace to be willing to be made willing to forgive when the time is ripe.

Don't let yourself off the hook until the day comes when you can let go – when you can drop the bitterness and resentment, the harshness and the hatred and open your hands to receive God's love for the person who has hurt you. Be aware that, as you let go, God comes to you to forgive you, lancing the abscess of negativity which has formed inside you through hatred.

20

Anywhere and everywhere

Reading: Psalm 100:2–5

Worship the Lord with gladness;
* come before him with joyful songs.*
Know that the Lord is God.
* It is he who made us, and we are his;*
we are his people, the sheep of his pasture.

Enter his gates with thanksgiving
* and his courts with praise;*
* give thanks to him and praise his name.*
For the Lord is good and his love
* endures for ever;*
his faithfulness continues through all generations.

Practising the presence of God simply means to be attentive, however momentarily, to the truth of Acts 17:28 that God is never far from any of us. In him we live and move and have our being. It is an awareness of and an in-tuneness with his loving presence.

I sometimes think of it in this way. Now that I am living overseas, I seem to have a deep need to keep in touch with England so I am grateful that the World Service of the BBC transmits regular programmes throughout the day and night. All I have to do is to tune my radio and I am connected to the homeland. God similarly transmits messages at all times: messages of unending love. To connect ourselves to this love, we need only fine-tune our hearts and minds to be aware of it. Then, no matter what we are doing, we can be drawn into deep mysteries: that God exists, that love is what he is, that he cares about us, that he is always working on our behalf, that he stooped to enter our world – stooped to enter our lives: that he indwells us. As David Adam puts it, 'we may vibrate to' his presence.

The Quaker Thomas Kelly calls this equal alertness to the sacred and the secular 'living concurrently'. He claims that we can train ourselves to be equally aware of the world in which we live and of God's presence. Likening us to the tortoise, he throws out this challenge: 'The tortoise swims about in the waters of the lake, but her mind is fixed to where her eggs are laid on the bank. So, do all the work of the world, but keep your mind in God.'

This concept inspired me when I was attending a Communion Service on one occasion. The service had scarcely begun when a little friend of mine aged nearly three decided that she would prefer my company to her mother's. So I spent the entire service living concurrently. On one level I was paying careful attention to Miriam's quiet (and not-so-quiet) chatter, drawing pictures for her, reading to her. On another level, my attention remained fully on the liturgy. The two experiences did not vie with each other; they dovetailed and even fed each other.

In similar vein, most of us spend much of our time thinking, even talking to ourselves – as we walk, as we work, as we fall asleep, as we wake – particularly when we are angry or anxious. Since this is so, tuning in to the ever-present love of God demands little more than a re-channelling of this ceaseless chatter so that we talk to the indwelling God as well as to ourselves.

Finding God everywhere

In *Dialogue with God*, Mark Virkler describes how he has worked at this life-changing discipline so that now, as he drives, he worships: 'I share love with Jesus, I sing Him a love song and allow Him to speak back to me in spontaneous thoughts.'

It took a personal crisis to convince the contemporary writer, Sue Monk Kidd, that God comes to us in the ordinary things of life. In *God's Joyful Surprise* she allows us to peep through the window of her own life:

> *Every day the nearness of God collected in me like rain water. I sensed Him coming and coming and coming . . . in a sound, a smell, a touch, a movement, in common things that shaped my day . . . I would stare at the most mundane things and be aware of His love. A pitcher of milk in the refrigerator, an old sweater, the steam rising off my soup, a quiet sky, an uprooted tree . . . all were gifts of love. 'Enjoy. Drink Me in,' [God] seemed to say. 'Find My love everywhere!'*

These authors have not suddenly stumbled on a new dimension of spirituality. They have simply woken up to the fact that when Jesus said, 'I will never leave you,' he meant it.[1]

Reflection

Jesus encouraged us to contemplate ordinary, everyday things to show us what God and his Kingdom are like and to reveal to us how they come. Things like a Middle

Eastern woman sweeping her house, a pearl, a good shepherd, sheep, sparrows, lilies, a mustard seed. God still reveals his nature, his love and his longing through mundane things.

To contemplate means to look at from a whole variety of angles, but it need not take long. When you can carve out of your busy life three or four minutes, gaze at what lies before you: a panoramic view of London, maybe, a photograph or a favourite painting, a crushed flower or a beggar. Or . . .

Ask yourself four questions:

What is God saying through this object or view?
What is God saying *to me*?
How might I feel if I could 'become' that thing?
How do I want to respond to God?

What does the sentence: 'In him we live and move and have our being' convey to you? What helps you to be aware of this reality? What makes it difficult?

Ponder these invitations:

Jesus said:

- contemplate the way the wildflowers grow (Luke 12:27), let the mystery remind you that God is your Provider,
- watch the birds (Luke 12:24), let them show you how much God values you,
- focus on the plight of the poor, let it put you in touch with the compassion of God,
- give food to the hungry, you'll be feeding me (Matthew 25:3 1ff),

- The Psalmist begs us to gaze at the sky, to let it give us glimpses of God's glory (Psalm 19).

So ask God to make you more aware.

Praying the 'Jesus Prayer'

Reading: Mark 10:46–52

Then they came to Jericho. As Jesus and his disciples, together with a large crowd, were leaving the city, a blind man, Bartimaeus (that is, the son of Timaeus), was sitting by the roadside begging. When he heard that it was Jesus of Nazareth, he began to shout, 'Jesus, Son of David, have mercy on me!'

Many rebuked him and told him to be quiet, but he shouted all the more, 'Son of David, have mercy on me!'

'What do you want me to do for you?' Jesus asked him.

The blind man said, 'Rabbi, I want to see.'

'Go,' said Jesus, 'your faith has healed you.' Immediately he received his sight and followed Jesus along the road.

The 'Jesus Prayer' is a deceptively simple yet peculiarly powerful prayer which is a derivation of the prayer Bartimaeus prayed; a prayer that has been valued and prayed by innumerable members of the Orthodox Church down the centuries. The full prayer consists of the words, 'Lord Jesus Christ, Son of God, have mercy on me, a sinner', but it is often shortened to 'Lord Jesus Christ, have mercy', 'Lord Jesus', or simply 'Jesus'.

'Jesus.' That is the key word, and the power of the prayer lies in this name which is above every other name. As the hymn-writer expressed it:

Jesus, the name high over all
In heaven or earth or sky
Angels and men before it fall
And devils fear and fly.

Jesus the name that calms our fears
And bids our sorrow cease
'Tis music in the sinner's ears
And life and health and peace.

I use the abbreviated version of this prayer as I turn from the busyness and attempt to enter the grand silence of God. As I breathe in, I whisper the name: 'Je' and as I breathe out, I complete the name: 'sus'. Praying in this way, I find, brings me back to that still point where God is most easily met and where his voice is most clearly heard. I do not use the Saviour's name lightly or as a mantra but rather as I might gently call a friend's name if I were entering their house – just to announce my arrival and to assure them that I am present to them.

Increasingly, as I pray the prayer in this way, I find it rising from my heart like a well-spring – as I work, as I fall asleep, when I wake. Like the pendulum of a grandfather clock, it reminds me what the pace of my life should be. Like gravitational pull, it draws me from a spinning-top lifestyle into deep-down, hushed stillness. When I am walking, I slow down so that the rhythm of my footsteps keeps time with the rhythm of the full version of the prayer; when I am resting or sitting at my desk, the prayer seems to rock inside me like the gentle movement of a boat or a rocking-chair.

Kallistos Ware, in *The Power of the Name*, points out that the joy of the Jesus Prayer is that it may be said, once or many times, in the scattered moments which otherwise would be spiritually wasted: when occupied with some familiar and semi-automatic task, such as dressing, washing up, mending socks, or digging in the garden; when walking or driving, when waiting in a bus queue or a traffic jam; in a moment of quiet before some especially painful or difficult interview; when unable to sleep or before we have gained full consciousness on waking. Part of the distinctive value of the Jesus Prayer lies precisely in the fact that, because of its radical simplicity, it can be prayed in conditions of distraction when more complex forms of prayer are impossible. It is especially helpful in moments of tension and grave anxiety.

I find that I can even pray this prayer while I am ploughing through a pile of paperwork or engrossed in a piece of creative writing. While concentrating on the task in hand, the prayer continues to sway inside me giving rise, very often, to a sense that God is with me – so close that I sometimes sense him by my side.

Reflection

Wherever you are at the moment, close your eyes and pray the Jesus Prayer slowly and quietly and several times. Either pray the full prayer:

> *Lord Jesus Christ, Son of God,*
> *Have mercy on me, a sinner.*

Or pray an abbreviation: '*Lord Jesus Christ . . . have mercy '. . .' Jesus.*'

In the middle of today's busyness, from time to time, pray the prayer again – while you wash up, while you clean your teeth, while you travel to work.

When you listen to the news or watch the television, repeat the prayer, changing it slightly: 'Lord Jesus Christ, have mercy on . . .' placing the names of individuals or countries or communities in the space.

When you read the newspaper, cut out pictures of people or situations you want to pray for. Place them beside the prayer: 'Lord Jesus Christ, have mercy on . . .'

Notice what happened to Bartimaeus when he prayed that prayer. Tell God what you expect to happen when you pray:

22

Through people

Reading: Ruth 2:2–10

Ruth the Moabitess said to Naomi, 'Let me go to the fields and pick up the leftover grain behind anyone in whose eyes I find favour.' Naomi said to her, 'Go ahead, my daughter.' So she went out and began to glean in the fields behind the harvesters. As it turned out, she found herself working in a field belonging to Boaz, who was from the clan of Elimelech.

Just then Boaz arrived from Bethlehem and greeted the harvesters, 'The Lord be with you!'

'The Lord bless you!' they called back.

Boaz asked the foreman of his harvesters, 'Whose young woman is that?'

The foreman replied, 'She is the Moabitess who came back from Moab with Naomi. She said, "Please let me glean and gather among the sheaves behind the harvesters." She went into the field and has worked steadily from morning till now, except for a short rest in the shelter.'

So Boaz said to Ruth, 'My daughter, listen to me. Don't go and glean in another field and don't go away from here. Stay here with my servant girls. Watch the field where the men are harvesting, and follow along after the girls. I have told the men not to touch you. And whenever you are thirsty, go and get a drink from the water jars the men have filled.'

At this, she bowed down with her face to the ground.

She exclaimed, 'Why have I found such favour in your eyes that you notice me – a foreigner?'

A smile is a powerful means of communication. This was underlined for me several years ago when I was a patient in a primitive hospital in what was then Yugoslavia. I had sustained head and back injuries in a car crash. Strangers had found me at the scene of the wreckage, noticed the blood seeping from a head wound and driven me as fast as their little Fiat would take us to the nearest hospital. There they placed me in the hands of the one doctor who could speak a smattering of English.

After the doctor had stitched up my head, I was wheeled into a ward of women who clearly spoke no English. I realised this as I was lifted from the trolley on to the makeshift bed in the corner of the ward. Five pairs of brown eyes scrutinised me, and five people plied me with questions. When I failed to respond, they raised their voices, as though speaking louder would enable me to reply in their native tongue. Eventually they gave up. The questions subsided but I sensed they continued to talk about me. That was hardly surprising: crowned as I was with bandages, I must have looked a comical spectacle. Perhaps they were even a little frightened that a foreigner had invaded the privacy of their ward.

Just as they gazed at me, so I gazed at them; and I noticed that each of my fellow-patients was elderly. All of them sat in bed, propped by pillows. The white pillow slips, white sheets and whitewashed walls made fitting frames for those olive, lined, leathery, weather-beaten faces.

As they chatted to each other that evening, I wondered

whether we would ever find anything in common. I wondered, too, what had become of my husband and children. None of them had been injured and I had last seen them rescuing our belongings from the overturned Dormobile in which we had been travelling from the Greek mainland when the accident occurred. Did they know where I was? Would they ever find me?

Such uncertainty, added to the strangeness of my surroundings, could have plunged me into the depths of despair. Instead, two things kept me calm. One was something I saw when the women in the ward were given their supper. The other was the curious power of a smile.

Supper came in the form of a goulash which was served from a galvanised bucket on to tin plates. For some reason I was not given anything to eat that evening but, out of the corner of my eyes, I watched my fellow-patients accept from the orderly their portion and some bread. Before any of them began to eat they signed themselves with the sign of the cross. My heart leapt for joy. This was a communist country, yet here I was locked in with five women who, it would seem, had not lost their faith in God. Their way of giving thanks for their food gave me the assurance that, just as God was in control of their lives, so he was in control of mine.

The ward was poorly lit by one bare light bulb dangling from the ceiling. The patients were responsible for turning out this light at night. After the supper things had been cleared away, they prepared themselves for bed. But before she switched off the light, the peasant woman in the bed next to mine shuffled over to my bedside, stood beside me, patted my hand and smiled before gently stooping down to kiss the small part of my forehead that was not covered in bandages. Then, one by one, the other four followed her example.

The two blankets on my bed were threadbare and thin, but suddenly I felt warm inside. Those five smiles brought a warmth no blanket can bring: the warmth of a comfort and care which makes physical pain bearable and shines through the dark clouds of fear and loneliness.

That was Good Friday. Next day, my husband and children found me. They brought with them one of the few personal belongings they had been able to salvage from the carcass of the Dormobile: my Bible. As I thumbed through it, an Easter card fell from its pages. It had been given to me before I left England – a simple card carrying a picture of the empty tomb.

On Easter Sunday morning, when the woman in the next bed came over to mine with her now-familiar smile and reassuring kiss, I showed her this card. She took one look at it and began to clap with the excitement of a delighted child. The others, curious, crowded round her. When they saw the card, they too grinned from ear to ear, clapped joyfully and cried out, '*Christus, Christus*,' pointing to me as though surprised that, like them, I believed in the Resurrection. I smiled back, relishing the fact that not only had we met on common ground, we had gone further and experienced an unspoken oneness in Christ; and all through a card and some smiles. It was the most memorable Easter gift I have ever been given.[1]

Reflection

Sometimes, when life is particularly bleak, we can lose all sense of the presence and love of God. At such times, God frequently chooses to come to us through the care and kindness of a friend – as he sent Boaz to Ruth and as he sent these women to me. Think of occasions when people have supported you in some way – through a letter, maybe, or a timely telephone call. Make a note of the way in which they helped and supported you so that you can cherish and learn

from them, then thank God for these reminders of
his love:

Recall occasions when you have been privileged to love
others in this way. Let all these memories give birth to a
prayer which you write or say:

23

Through a doctor or a nurse

Reading: John 13:2–9

The evening meal was being served . . . Jesus knew that the Father had put all things under his power, and that he had come from God and was returning to God; so he got up from the meal, took off his outer clothing, and wrapped a towel round his waist. After that, he poured water into a basin and began to wash his disciples' feet, drying them with the towel that was wrapped round him.

He came to Simon Peter, who said to him, 'Lord, are you going to wash my feet?'

Jesus replied, 'You do not realise now what I am doing, but later you will understand.'

'No,' said Peter, 'you shall never wash my feet.'

Jesus answered, 'Unless I wash you, you have no part with me.'

'Then, Lord,' Simon Peter replied, 'not just my feet but my hands and my head as well!'

I have no idea how long my operation lasted. What I do know is that, later that evening, as I regained consciousness, I heard someone groaning. I also remember feeling shocked when I discovered that the person was me. I was still lying on the trolley and two nurses were with me, saying, soothingly, 'It's all over. It's all over now.' I remember the tenderness of their touch as they lifted me from the trolley to my bed. And I remember the gentleness and understanding tone of their voice. But apart from recalling the frightening feeling of thirst, I can recall nothing more of Thursday – the night of the operation. But I remember Friday.

Throughout Thursday night, I was given pain-killing injections so I experienced little discomfort and by six o'clock on Friday morning, I was wide awake. The night sister, Lucy Wong, and Dolly, her colleague, had clearly been keeping an eye on me all night because, as soon as they saw that I was awake, they helped me out of bed, and helped me reach the wash-basin in my room where I was able to refresh myself by washing my face. Painstakingly, and taking care not to touch the sensitive area around my wound, they then washed my entire body, discarded the blood-stained hospital gown and invited me to choose which of my clean nightdresses I would most like to wear. They then helped me back into bed where, lying back on the freshly plumped-up pillows, I registered, with amazement, that I felt remarkably well.

To prevent me experiencing the nausea which can be so distressing to patients who are recovering from a general anaesthetic, I had been warned that I would be given no food or drink until Sunday. This posed only one problem: 'My throat feels so dry and my lips are parched,' I complained to Lucy. 'Have you any lip lotion?' she asked. It had not occurred to me to bring any with me so Lucy disappeared and returned a few minutes later clutching a small jar of her own lip balm. 'From the Body Shop,' she explained, grinning broadly. 'Try spreading some on your lips.' The lotion was balm indeed: soothing and effective. Almost immediately, the dryness disappeared from my lips. I was not only relieved but deeply touched by Lucy's generosity and thoughtfulness.

As I have reflected on the quality of care I received that day and on subsequent days, I have frequently likened it to the kind of love Jesus gave to his disciples: the kind of love which he expressed, in particular, during the Last Supper when he washed his disciples' dirty, sweaty feet. Commenting on this moving piece of the Master's ministry, Sheila Cassidy observes that it was on this occasion supremely that Jesus demonstrated the fact that 'the love of God must be cashed out in love of neighbour'; that life and love are about service and sacrifice; that love pours out its life for another. 'And life is not just blood given once and for all, it is time and energy, tears and laughter, poured out hourly, daily, over a lifetime.'

She goes on to tell of an occasion when she visited the L'Arche Community in France. Her visit coincided with Holy Week and, on Maundy Thursday, the community sat in a huge circle in the centre of which sat Patrick, one of the helpers, and Michel, one of the mentally handicapped. Beside them lay a towel and basin.

During the sermon, Sheila observed Michel poised impatiently waiting for the moment when he would be permitted to wash Patrick's feet:

His eyes were fixed on the water and he held the towel in readiness. At last he was allowed to begin. No silver jug and basin here . . . This was the real thing: a washing up bowl, full of warm soapy water with Patrick's foot plunged firmly in. Lovingly, Michel soaped it, up and down and round the heel and then gently between each toe. At last, he was satisfied, and lifted it out onto his lap to dry. Gently he patted the clean skin and separated the toes, drying each one individually. Then the other foot was soaped, rinsed and dried with equal care . . . Here was the carer being tended by his charge. Here was Michel, the simpleton, showing us how to love. It was not just the gentleness, but the rapt concentration and attention to detail. He was showing us in his own way that

people are precious, that the human body is wondrously
beautiful, to be honoured and handled with care.[1]

What Michel had done for Patrick, Sister Lucy and Dolly
were doing for me.[2]

Reflection
Try to picture the three scenes painted above: Jesus taking
a bowl and towel and washing his disciples' feet, Michel
painstakingly washing Patrick's feet, and Sister Lucy and
Dolly reverencing my body. Have you ever watched
anyone else being cherished in this way? Or can you
think of occasions when people have served you like this?
Who were they? How did it feel? Relive the memories
and write a prayer out of the experience:

What opportunities do you have to wash other people's
feet, metaphorically speaking? Ask God to give you the
grace to give others time and energy, tears and laughter,
a listening ear or love expressed in practical ways.

Pray particularly today for people in the caring professions as they wash others' feet. And ask God to show you if there are people to whom you can minister in this way. Jot down any names that come to mind:

24

Through loving others

Reading: Matthew 25:31–40

'When the Son of Man comes in his glory, and all the angels with him, he will sit on his throne in heavenly glory. All the nations will be gathered before him, and he will separate the people one from another as a shepherd separates the sheep from the goats. He will put the sheep on his right and the goats on his left.

'Then the King will say to those on his right, "Come, you who are blessed by my Father; take your inheritance . . . For I was hungry and you gave me something to eat, I was thirsty and you gave me something to drink, I was a stranger and you invited me in, I needed clothes and you clothed me, I was sick and you looked after me, I was in prison and you came to visit me."

'Then the righteous will answer him, "Lord, when did we see you hungry and feed you, or thirsty and give you something to drink? When did we see you a stranger and invite you in, or needing clothes and clothe you? When did we see you sick or in prison and go to visit you?"

'The King will reply, "I tell you the truth, whatever you did for one of the least of these brothers of mine, you did for me."'

In this parable, Jesus seems to be persuading us that when hurting people weep, he weeps; when people starve, he starves; when people are crushed by cruelty, he is crushed.

A dream once helped me to drink in the significance of this parable. In my dream I saw a tramp stagger through my garden gate. He was dressed in dirty, tattered clothes and was clearly unwell and weak. I watched him bend over my herb garden; I heard him vomit. My heart went out to him. I felt great warmth for him: I wanted to go to him, to help him, but before I could move, I woke up.

Although I was awake, the dream remained as vivid as ever – the tramp still seemed real. So I talked to God about what I had seen: 'Lord, you know that I'm not normally like that. The real me would have been angry if that had happened. Why was I so different in my dream?'

'In your dream, you reached the heart of the matter,' came the reply. 'I was the tramp. You sensed this. That is why you saw, not the tattered clothing, but me; that is why you were concerned, not with the smell and the mess, but with the person. When you felt warmth for that tramp and wanted to go to him, you were feeling warmth for me. Learn to live as you reacted in your dream.'

That dream helped me to appreciate the meaning of St Teresa of Avila's claim, 'Though we do not have our Lord with us in bodily presence, we have our neighbour, who, for the ends of love and loving service, is as good as our Lord himself.'

It also helped me to identify with Henri Nouwen's claim that, 'The hunger of the poor, the torture of prisoners, the threat of war in many countries, and the immense human suffering we hear about from all directions can call us to a deeply human response . . . if we are willing to see in the brokenness of our fellow human beings the brokenness of God.' I felt I understood what he meant when he continues, 'God's brokenness does not repulse. It attracts.' It attracts because, as we sense the agony of God's loved ones, we sense the agony of God himself.

I was pondering these mysteries as I travelled to London one day. While I was sitting in the cafeteria at St Pancras station, waiting for the home-bound train, I became aware of two people – a man and a woman – creating a disturbance a few tables away from me. The man resembled the tramp in my dream. He was trying, in a rough but concerned way, to comfort the woman who was clearly distressed.

When her companion went to fetch her a drink, I had an uninterrupted view of this woman. She looked as though she was in her late fifties. Her hair was falling out in places and her white, lined face bore the marks of intolerable suffering. Although it was a cold day in March, she was scantily dressed and she was shaking uncontrollably.

As I watched her, I felt for her the same love I had felt for the tramp in my dream. Quite involuntarily, I found myself weeping for her. As the tears rolled down my cheeks and into my coffee, I noticed that she was staring at me. Our eyes met. We sat gazing at each other for several seconds. I trusted that the compassion I felt for her would be reflected in my eyes and face. Tentatively, I smiled at her. She looked surprised at first, but eventually she smiled back. I noticed that she stopped shaking. Her companion returned with a drink and something for her to eat. As she ate, she looked frequently over to my table – smiling every time.

A few days later, I was meditating on the way Mary anointed Jesus just before his death. I sensed that her generous gesture of pouring precious ointment over Jesus's head had also poured new strength into his spirit, the strength he needed as he embarked on the last lap of his journey – that most painful week of his earthly life. 'Just as Mary poured strength into me, so you poured strength into that needy woman in London,' a still, small voice whispered. 'You strengthened her for the next lap of her painful journey through life and when you poured strength into her, you poured it into me also.'[1]

Reflection

Many people have discovered that, the more they soak up the love of God through their prayer, the more they find themselves drawn to human pain as though by a magnet. The closer they come to God in prayer, the more they understand the connection between pain on our planet and God's pain, and they become highly motivated to alleviate some of this pain and suffering. Reflect on your own reaction to pictures of the homeless or the starving you see staring up at you from the pages of newspapers or magazines or out of the television screen. Or think of the way you feel when you see people begging in the streets. Reflect, too, on Jesus's claim, 'Whatever you did for one of the least of these brothers of mine, you did for me.' Let your reflection give birth to a prayer or a poem:

Ask God to show you how you can pour strength into him by pouring strength into one or more of his hurting people. Record what you sense he is saying:

25

Through intercession

Reading: James 2:14–19

What good is it, my brothers, if a man claims to have faith but has no deeds? Can such faith save him? Suppose a brother or sister is without clothes and daily food. If one of you says to him, 'Go, I wish you well; keep warm and well fed,' but does nothing about his physical needs, what good is it? In the same way, faith by itself, if it is not accompanied by action, is dead. But someone will say, 'You have faith; I have deeds.'

Show me your faith without deeds, and I will show you my faith by what I do.

The briefest of glances at the Gospels reveals that, when Jesus walked this earth, there was a particular group of people he cared about: the poor. As Jean Vanier, himself a champion of the poor, puts it: 'It is as though he is attracted in a special way, almost like a magnet, to those who are suffering, or broken or rejected.'[1] It follows that when we find ourselves being drawn closer and closer to Jesus, we shall also find ourselves becoming more and more concerned for the poor. To be with Jesus is to be in the presence of love and compassion. This compassion is contagious: it will rub off on us and overflow from us, and we will find ourselves asking: 'Who, for me, are the poor?'

I once asked a friend and mentor that question. His answer surprised and challenged me: 'Don't we discover the answer to that question by asking, "How am I poor?"'

The question intrigued me and made me think and, like many such questions, helped me to move forward. I was standing at one of life's crossroads at the time, sensing that the finger of God was beckoning me to become involved with the poor in some way. When I asked myself the question: 'How am I poor?' the answer rose from somewhere within me:

My poverty, so often, is a poverty of spirit. I write about prayer as relationship with God and attempt, on retreats and Quiet Days, to lead others to the Fountain of Life, Jesus, but sometimes I do it from the barrenness which can be born of busyness so I feel as though I am scraping the bottom of an empty barrel.

It was a humbling moment and an important one. Other Christians in leadership, I know full well, suffer from the same dis-ease – particularly Christians who live and work overseas where the resources that people in the West take for granted are so few and far between. As I faced my own poverty, I also found the answer to the question: 'Who, for me, are the poor?'

I not only found the answer to my question, I also discovered the nature of my new vocation. I now work full-time with my 'poor' – those who have given everything they have and are for the extension of Christ's Kingdom overseas. Together with my husband, I now have the privilege of leading prayer retreats for them where we seek to take them by the hand, as it were, and stay alongside them in love as they feast on food no money can buy – the banquet of *God's* love.[2]

It has been my privilege to visit many such people in the countries which they have adopted – people who could be climbing the professional ladder in their home country, people who could be lining their pockets with the world's gold, but who have chosen, instead, to live and work quietly in parts of the world where the only thing they can do for Christ is to incarnate his love and pray.

The only thing they can do? Yes. Sometimes, such people see little apparent fruit for their love and their labour. In the countries where they work, they do not enjoy the kudos of seeing thousands flock to meetings they speak at. Indeed, there are no meetings – just a day-in, day-out rhythm of prayer and overflowing love. Often they feel spiritually drained and dry. Sometimes they wonder how effective they are. Sometimes the only sign that God is working through them is that, when they pray, they weep and they groan as they confront the darkness in which their part of the world is enveloped. Rather, I should say, the Holy Spirit weeps through them in the way Paul describes:

> *The Spirit helps us in our weakness. We do not know what we ought to pray for, but the Spirit himself inter-cedes for us with groans that words cannot express . . . [and] in accordance with God's will. (Romans 8: 26–7)*

They groan with the Spirit because the going seems so hard, because people's hearts seem so hard and the sense of oppression hangs over them like a thick and menacing cloud. And yet they stay and they pray and they work and they love just as Jesus before them stayed and prayed and worked and loved.

But, of course, we need only to pack our bags and travel overseas if we hear a clear call from God to do so. It is equally possible to work in this hidden way in our own home country. Those of us who do work overseas often testify to sensing the power of the prayer of our supporters, some of whom intercede for us spasmodically, some regularly – like the friends who have our engagement diary tucked into their Bibles or pinned on their notice-boards. When some of them write to tell us of the times and ways in which the Holy Spirit has prayed through them or inspired them to pray, the timeliness and aptness of these letters trigger within me tears of gratitude – to God for his faithfulness in raising up such prayer partners, and to them for their openness to the Spirit.

And the mystery is that it is while we pray, with groans and tears, entering into the cost and pain of it all, we are being encountered by God. We may not feel, see or hear him but he is there prompting our prayer, praying in us and through us and answering our prayers in the way which seems best to his eternal plan.

Reflection

Ask yourself the question: 'How am I poor?' Ask God to show you the answer to it. Does this point you in the direction of the way in which you could be touching some of the world's poor?

Re-read the verses from James's epistle. Think of occasions when you have been in the presence of the wealthy and the impoverished, the popular or famous and the shy and the unknown. How have you reacted? How might James have commented on this reaction?

In future, when you intercede, try to be aware that, in intercession, we are drawing alongside the Great Intercessor, Jesus himself. Try to be aware that being an intercessor is costly in terms of time and emotion, energy and tears, but that God is there, praying through you by his Spirit and interpreting your sighs and groans.

Tell God how it feels to be encountered by him in this way:

26

Through Holy Communion

Reading: Matthew 26:26–29

While they were eating, Jesus took bread, gave thanks and broke it, and gave it to his disciples, saying, 'Take and eat; this is my body.'

Then he took the cup, gave thanks and offered it to them, saying, 'Drink from it, all of you. This is my blood of the covenant, which is poured out for many for the forgiveness of sins. I tell you, I will not drink of this fruit of the vine from now on until that day when I drink it anew with you in my Father's kingdom.'

I woke up feeling refreshed and admitted to my husband on the telephone that I was looking forward to attending the service of Holy Communion in the chapel at 5.15 p.m. When I mentioned this longing to Sister Thomas she simply asked: 'Do you think it's really wise to go down to the chapel, dear? It's not yet three full days since your operation. Why not let me arrange for you to receive the sacrament in the quietness of your own room?'

My initial reaction was one of disappointment; I had so looked forward to drinking in the stillness of the chapel.

But when I reflected on the questions I had been asked, I sensed the wisdom which lay behind them. I had only just started to eat again and so far had walked no farther than the toilet which was situated within a few yards of my room. To reach the chapel would necessitate a journey in the lift and a much longer walk along the length of the ground floor. By the time I reached the chapel, I would probably feel so exhausted that I would scarcely benefit from the liturgy or the spiritual feast concealed in the bread and the wine. Instead, I settled myself in my prayer corner, grateful that it would be possible to listen to the entire service on the hospital radio and that, eventually, the sacrament would be brought to me by the chaplain.

As I listened to the readings and the liturgy being relayed from the chapel, I felt far from God; so much so that I burst into tears. While I waited for the chaplain, I pictured him standing outside the chapel greeting, in turn, each of the patients who had attended the service. And I listened to two tapes: a song which had been given to me in New Zealand and another of those plaintive Taizé chants which I find draw me most easily into the felt presence of God. The song is called 'Come as you are'. It is sung by a Carmelite monk and God always seems to say personally to me what the monk is singing:

> Come as you are
> That's how I love you
> Come as you are
> Feel quite at home
> Nothing can change the love that I bear you
> All will be well, just come as you are.[1]

Those words triggered off more tears but this time they were healing tears rather than bitter ones, and as I played the Taizé chant: 'Stay here and keep watch with me', I noticed that a new sense of perspective and peace was stealing over me in rather the same way as the sun sometimes breaks through seemingly solid thunder clouds and then spreads its light and warmth over everything in sight.

By the time the chaplain came, a sense of inner calm had been restored. Still sitting in my armchair, I was gazing at Rublev's *Icon of the Holy Trinity*. This icon is sometimes called *A Circle of Love* because the three persons of the Godhead are sitting in a circle. On the right-hand side of the circle sits God the Holy Spirit. His head has been painted in such a way that it points to Jesus who is sitting at the centre of the circle. Jesus, in turn, gazes at his Father as though he is saying, 'Let me take you into his presence.' I prayed now, wordlessly, that the Holy Spirit would take me to the Father. I gazed at the empty place at the table which Rublev has painted and longed that I might take my place at that table where a chalice reminds us that the Son sacrificed his life on the Cross of Calvary, such was his love for the world.

As the chaplain placed into my hands first the wafer and then the silver chalice which contained the wine, I ate and drank with gratitude. Because of the place I have reached on my own spiritual journey, the service of Holy Communion is of vital importance to me and though I doubt that I shall ever fully understand precisely what Jesus meant when he told us that the bread we receive is his body and the wine his blood, what I do know is that, in some mysterious, mystical way, these elements are nutritious; as essential to my spiritual well-being as food and drink are to my body.

What I also discovered, as this short, powerful service progressed, was that, though my ability to concentrate on words was severely limited, prayers like the prayer of absolution seemed wonderfully liberating, prayed, as they so obviously were by this chaplain, with deep conviction and sincerity.

When the chaplain left me, I lingered in my prayer corner where once again I tuned in to the powerful sense of Christ's presence which had so often seemed to fill this room. Even when Sister Thomas came to take my temperature and check my pulse, the silence was not broken: it was as profound as ever. Because she knows how to be not only active in contemplation but contemplative in action, her presence never felt intrusive. On the contrary, her presence always seemed to embody a little of the sheltering love of the God who cares.[2]

Reflection

What do you understand by Jesus's words: 'This is my body . . . This is my blood'? Write a letter to God expressing your thoughts and feelings:

How do you respond to Jesus's invitation: 'Take and eat. Drink'? Do you ever recoil from accepting these treasures? Do you sometimes receive them casually without really thinking through the implications of what you are doing? Or . . .? As you think about the question, tell God how you would like to approach these very special love gifts:

How do you prepare yourself to attend the service of Holy Communion? Bearing in mind the nature of this particular service, how would you like to prepare?

27

By the grace of God's Spirit

Reading: John 14:15–17; 16:7, 13, 14

If you love me, you will obey what I command. And I will ask the Father, and he will give you another Counsellor to be with you for ever – the Spirit of truth. The world cannot accept him, because it neither sees him nor knows him. But you know him, for he lives with you and will be in you . . . It is for your good that I am going away. Unless I go away, the Counsellor will not come to you; but if I go, I will send him to you . . . When he, the Spirit of truth, comes, he will guide you into all truth. He will not speak on his own; he will speak only what he hears, and he will tell you what is yet to come. He will bring glory to me by taking from what is mine and making it known to you.

The Holy Spirit is, first and foremost, a person. As Jesus puts it, he is a counsellor, a comforter, and an advocate. He guides us and speaks to us, convinces and constrains us, transforms and warns us. He can be grieved and lied against. He is not just any person. He is the third person of the Holy Trinity who, from all eternity, has emanated from God the Father and God the Son. As someone has summarised the situation: 'He is the uncreated, creative power of the holy, loving God. He is personally present to but transcendently other than the human spirit.' Paul goes so far as to call him, not only God's Spirit (2 Corinthians 3:3) but God himself (2 Corinthians 3:17). His presence is made known to us by Jesus who refers to him as the Father's good gift (Luke 11:13).

Will I ever forget the evening when, in a friend's lounge, God gave me the graced moment where I was able to experience for myself that the Holy Spirit floods our hearts with God's love (Romans 5:5 JBP). The friend in whose home it happened had telephoned me to say that he believed he had been baptised with the Holy Spirit and that he had begun to pray in tongues. Struggling as I was at that time to be open to the Spirit of God while fearing such openness because of the eccentric behaviour of some 'charismatics', my initial response was 'Oh dear! Maybe we can talk about it on Monday after the meeting.'

The meeting had finished, everyone else had gone home and my friend had told me his story. The genuineness of his experience touched me and although I had gone to the meeting fully intending to 'sort him out' theologically, I knew that to dispute what he had told me would be an affront to him, a trusted friend, and to God. Instead, I simply reverenced his experience.

As we had done so often before, we then prayed together. As we prayed, I became aware of him gently and quietly praying in tongues. I became aware, too, at one stage, that he was laying his hands on my head very gently and asking God to touch me afresh. No rushing wind swept through the room and no tongues of flame hovered over our heads but gradually the lounge became holy ground as the sense of the presence and the love of God overshadowed me. As I reflected later, it was as though God was pouring into me liquid love. I could almost feel it being spread through every cell of my brain before it percolated around the inner recesses of my being.

The sensation stunned me, silenced me and thrilled me. When I left my friend's home and walked through the dark streets to my own, the love seemed to intensify and as I slipped into bed beside my husband, the love continued to overshadow and to overwhelm me. So far as I am aware, sleep eluded me that night but I was glad of the hushed darkness to absorb the elixir of love in a way I had never before envisaged, let alone experienced.

For days, although I carried on with my normal routine, I seemed strangely detached from it all. It was as though I was watching the world through double-glazed windows. Outside, my family and friends were acting normally; inside, I felt as though I was moving in a womb of love.

'I suppose this is what people call being "baptised with the Holy Spirit",' I said to my husband. He understood, though neither of us appreciated what we now know – that, as Andrew Murray described it one hundred years ago: 'The Spirit is nothing less than the Divine Love itself come down to dwell in us . . . The Spirit comes to us freighted with all the love of God and of Jesus: the Spirit is the Love of God . . . The outpouring of the Spirit is the inpouring of Love.'

When this love-shedding Spirit not only indwells us but also immerses us in love, he gives far more than the head-knowledge that God loves us intimately and uniquely. In Paul's words, he spreads God's love into the nooks and crannies of our lives until, in that love, we live and move and have our entire being.[1]

Reflection
People sometimes ask me why they rarely seem to sense the love of God. Is there something they can do to tune in to it, they ask. In Romans 5:5 Paul gives us one answer to

that question. There is a sense in which we can do nothing except to receive the grace of God through the ministry of his Holy Spirit. The third person of the Holy Trinity is the One who floods our hearts with an awareness of God's love. So, if you feel you can, write a prayer asking God to fill you afresh with his Spirit:

Just as Jesus breathed his Spirit into his disciples on the first Easter evening (John 20:19–23), invite him to breathe his life and his energy into you now.

Look back over the past twenty-four hours. As you watch an action replay of the events, ask the Holy Spirit to show you where he was at work in you – helping you, perhaps, to exercise more patience than usual, enabling you to act more lovingly than you normally do, giving you wisdom and discernment in tricky situations, freeing you to be gently confrontational. Ask him, too, to show you where you blocked his activity inside you – through stubbornness or disobedience or lack of co-operation. Make a note of the insights he gives you:

Over the coming weeks and months, repeat that exercise – daily, if possible. It is the sort of prayer work you can do as you commute or as you walk to the shops. In addition to giving you these insights, expect God the Holy Spirit to give you warnings, comfort and guidance and an awareness of the Father's love. When you catch glimpses of his activity inside you, give God the praise and the glory. When he highlights failures, let that be a challenge to grow, not an invitation to grovel.

28

When obeying

Reading: Matthew 26:36–46

Then Jesus went with his disciples to a place called Gethsemane, and he said to them, 'Sit here while I go over there and pray.' He took Peter and the two sons of Zebedee along with him, and he began to be sorrowful and troubled. Then he said to them, 'My soul is overwhelmed with sorrow to the point of death. Stay here and keep watch with me.'

Going a little farther, he fell with his face to the ground and prayed, 'My Father, if it is possible, may this cup be taken from me. Yet not as I will, but as you will.'

He went away a second time and prayed, 'My Father, if it is not possible for this cup to be taken away unless I drink it, may your will be done.'

When he came back, he again found [the disciples] sleeping, because their eyes were heavy. So he left them and went away once more and prayed the third time saying the same thing.

Then he returned to the disciples and said to them, 'Are you still sleeping and resting? Look, the hour is near, and the Son of Man is betrayed into the hands of sinners. Rise, let us go! Here comes my betrayer.'

Busyness was not the only hindrance to listening to God. It was the disobedience which seriously threatened my relationship with him. With shame, I now read my own accounts of my struggle to give God the mastery in certain relationships which were corroding my friendship with Jesus. I wanted the best of both worlds: my way and God's. When God faced me with the inevitable choice – my way *or* his, I squealed. For months I was so full of self-will that I heard little from the still, small voice of God. Bible meditation ceased, Bible study stopped. I would dip into the Bible from time to time but it communicated nothing. This was hardly surprising: I had not yet learned that God's Word is not simply to be studied, read or personalised – it has to be obeyed. But as William Barclay warns: 'There are people into whose minds [and emotions] the word has no more chance of gaining an entry than the seed has of settling into the ground that has been beaten hard by many feet.'[1]

There are many things which can close a person's mind. Disobedience is the most effective. As someone aptly said: 'The one who truly listens is also the one who truly obeys.'

It hurts to recall the failures. It is the kind of hurt I felt once when I watched a family on holiday on the beach. The parents were trying hard to give their children a happy holiday. The sun was shining, the sandy beach stretched for miles, white waves tickled the shore, but the children were squabbling over a small, red, plastic spade.

I was like those children. God's generosity to me had known no limits. Yet I was throwing his love back in his face because the attractions the world offered seemed to possess a greater magnetic power than the wonder of his presence. At times I rejected him altogether. At times I feared my life of listening to him was a closed chapter.

But the Holy Spirit continued to bombard my ears with messages from God: uncomfortable messages, disconcerting messages, messages which troubled me and caused me to struggle to survive. I would hear these messages and take careful note of them, and I would respond to them in my prayer journal, not recognising that the Spirit's work is not always to notify us of God's love but rather to bring us up with a jolt: lovingly to show us his displeasure. Slowly and thoughtfully I made a reappraisal of my life: where I was going, what I was wanting, what God was asking of me. Anything which obstructed the path would have to go. Equally slowly, but quite deliberately, I cleared out the clutter which had kept me from Christ.

I now see what was happening. God emptied me of so much of self that he created within me a greater capacity for him. He had read the signs which showed that, at the deepest level of my being, this was what I wanted. When my Bible lay unused, a hunger would grow inside me. When my prayer time became nothing more than good and evil waging war within, a holy dissatisfaction filled me. It gave birth to the realisation that I cannot live without him, that a life devoid of listening to him, loving him and being met by him spells emptiness and not fullness. The good would therefore have to win.

Obedience, I know, is the key, the 'Open sesame' to listening. For years God engraved that word on my heart. I know that disobedience can lock and bolt the door against God's still, small voice.

But God's patience seems infinite. When I do obey, I become freshly and wondrously aware of God's life-springs welling up within me. That is hardly surprising since God is never reluctant to come to our aid but responds gladly to every advance of ours. The joy of surrendering to him is usually sweet: a privilege. And being found, held and loved by God all over again, and receiving his activity deep into the inner recesses of my being fills me with fresh awe and wonder and praise. The encounter is usually so powerful that it leaves me asking the question. '*Why* don't I heed Mary's advice when she says: "Do whatever he tells you"?'[2]

Reflection

Think of occasions when you have been resisting God's voice and love; when you have been disobeying him. What happened to your relationship with him? How did you feel? How would you describe yourself?

Think of occasions in the scriptures when someone's obedience is described. How do you sense they felt? How do you sense God felt? How do you feel when you have done a U-turn – walking away from self and towards Jesus?

There is a sense in which our conversion to Christ is gradual and not sudden. This is because our personality is made up of a variety of layers. Some of these layers have already been touched and changed by God. Others lie hidden, sometimes resistant. Ask God to show you when yet another layer of your personality needs to be touched and changed by him. Ask for the grace, not to resist, but to yield; to offer him 'the gold of obedience'.

Ask God to show you whether, at this moment, there are disobediences in your life he yearns to deal with. Give him the opportunity to respond to that question. Remembering that 'The Lord disciplines those he loves', if you can pray it with integrity, ask God to go on and on giving you the grace of obedience.

Lord, turn my whole being to your praise and glory.

29

Through sacrifice

Reading: Philippians 2:6–11
Christ Jesus
Who, being in very nature God,
 did not consider equality with God
 something to be grasped,
but made himself nothing,
 taking the very nature of a servant,
 being made in human likeness.
And being found in appearance as a man,
 he humbled himself
and became obedient to death – even death on a cross!
Therefore God exalted him to the highest place
 and gave him the name that is above every name,
that at the name of Jesus every knee should bow,
in heaven and on earth and under the earth,
and every tongue confess that Jesus Christ is Lord,
to the glory of God the Father.

When we serve God we are truly free because he created
us in such a way that we will only enjoy complete fulfilment
in life when we are reverencing him and everyone and

everything he has made, and when we are serving him and them. This lies at the very heart of who we are.

There is a snag, however. As children of our first parents, Adam and Eve, we have become victims of the Fall. Just as our first parents believed the big lie Satan whispered in their ears – that God is a spoilsport, out to deprive us of joy rather than to delight us with his love, so we are easily beguiled into believing in this caricature of God. This means that a civil war may frequently rage inside us. While some parts of our personality will struggle to be true to our calling, to serve Christ and the world, to serve Christ in the world, other parts of us will rebel and insist on putting self before our Master. One of the challenges which faces us, therefore, is to discern and to discipline those parts of ourselves which seem intent on ensuring that our world revolves around 'number one', self, rather than God.

That is not to imply, however, that the main initiative in winning this perennial battle is ours; it is not. God takes the initiative. I discovered this while I was on retreat on one occasion. One of the questions I had taken with me was: 'Lord, do you want me to go to live in Cyprus?' The answer came within the first few days of this five-week-long holiday with God. But the answer faced me with a bigger, more pressing question. Now that I felt as certain as I could that God was, indeed, calling me to make the island my base, the question was: 'How do I say "Yes" to this request?'

For weeks, I wrote eloquent prayers telling God that I wanted to say 'Yes.' I wrote a poem which brought into sharp focus my fears and longings now that I was confronted with the need to say 'Yes.' I even studied and meditated on the incarnation of Jesus in the hope that I would gain courage and inspiration from the example of the ready, generous, all-embracing 'Yes' which Mary uttered when the angel invited her to become the mother of the Messiah. Yet, although a burning desire to capitulate consumed me, no 'Yes' so much as squeezed through my lips.

It was on this retreat that I meditated on the word 'grace'. It was on this retreat that I fell asleep begging for a generous slice of this free gift. It was in the middle of the last night of this retreat, at three in the morning to be precise, that I awoke with a joyful, spontaneous 'Yes' rising from somewhere deep inside me.

As I look back on that retreat and read the pages of the prayer journal in which I was writing at the time, I notice that a word I used frequently was 'fear'. I was afraid of leaving the English home I loved for a much smaller house in a country where I would always be a foreigner who carried on her person an identity card marked ALIEN. I was afraid that, at a time when the world seemed gripped by recession, the financial support we would need would not be forthcoming. And I was afraid that, if I were stripped of all the support structures which I had taken for granted for years – the team who worked with me, my spiritual director and others who were there 'for me' whenever I needed them, the quiet places to which I could retreat when I needed a place 'just to be' with God – I would find myself unable to cope.

Others facing the enormity of the 'Yes' which confronts them have spoken to me of similar fears. They are not only natural, they are a gift because they reveal to us that, though we may have been claiming to find our security in God, we have, in fact, been seeking our security in our homes and our salaries, our roles and our successes. As Ronald Rolheiser points out, as human beings who are creatures of our culture, we spontaneously draw support from fame, hedonism, pleasure, power, possessions, sex and so on. When we are faced with counting the cost of the 'Yes' God wants us to whisper, we are brought face to face with our need to draw strength instead from the resources of God, through the 'littleness' of dependence on him and on his people.

As Jean Vanier puts it, with an incisiveness that never ceases to challenge me: 'We all have to choose between two ways of being crazy: the foolishness of the Gospel and the nonsense of the values of the world'.[1]

Reflection

Reflect on the passage from Philippians. Why do you think Jesus exchanged the glory of heaven and the wonder of his Father's presence for the squalor of earth? Tell him how you feel about his humility and self-sacrifice.

Reflect on Jean Vanier's claim, quoted above on this page. Which method of being crazy have you been choosing and why? Tell God which way you would like to choose. Tell him, too, what makes it difficult to take that path:

If you feel you can say it with integrity, pray this prayer:

Take, Lord,
and receive all my liberty,
my memory, my understanding
and my entire will,
all that I have and possess.

You have given all to me,
to you, Lord, I return it.

All is yours:
do with it what you will.
Give me only your love
and your grace,
that is enough for me.[2]

30

The eternal encounter

In Richard Attenborough's award-winning film, *Gandhi*, the cameras take us to a remote railway station in India. There we see a platform teeming with waiting Indians. Two British soldiers survey the scene from their hilltop vantage-point. Nodding towards the crowd as a steam train approaches, one asks: 'What are they doing? What are they waiting for?' His colleague replies: 'I've no idea. All I know is they received a telegram a few days ago. On it were three words: "He is coming."'

The train snorted to a halt. A small, middle-aged Indian dressed in white home-spun cloth alighted. The people surged forward to greet him. Dark eyes lit up, weary faces creased with smiles. And the soldiers mocked at the reverence with which this seeming insignificant native was being treated. Why the euphoria? Here was just another Indian, here today, gone tomorrow. Gone tomorrow? They were not to know that the charismatic figure, Gandhi, would one day lead his country into freedom from British rule. The thought had never even crossed their minds.

Neither can the world concede that our telegram from heaven has arrived. 'I am coming soon,' Jesus promises (Revelation 3:11). The world cannot detect the joy which wells up within us like a fountain as we read his further promise, 'I am making everything new!' (Revelation 21:5).

Has anyone captured the atmosphere more accurately

than C. S. Lewis as he concludes his famous Narnia tales? Here he claims that the things which happened to his characters after the books ended were so great and beautiful that he could not write them. Although for us it was the end of all the stories, for them it was the beginning of the real story.

> *All their life in this world and all their adventures in Narnia had only been the cover and the title page: now at last they were beginning Chapter One of the Great Story which no one on earth has read: which goes on for ever: in which every chapter is better than the one before.*[1]

In the book of Revelation, too, every chapter is more thrilling than the one before. Reading the book at one sitting is as tantalising as hearing the sound of running water when climbing in the mountains on a hot summer's day, and as thirst-quenching as drinking long draughts from such crystal-clear streams. Each promise is precious: the promise of 'a new heaven and a new earth', the promise that God will 'wipe away every tear from [our] eyes', the promise that 'death shall be no more, and never again shall there be sorrow or crying or pain' (21:1–4). But the greatest thrill of all will be that we shall see the Beloved face to face. He will make his home with us and we with him. We shall be his people and he will be with us. We shall delight, not in his presents, but in his everlasting presence.

And, for the first time in our lives, we shall be set free truly to worship. Some of us have already received a foretaste of what the worship of heaven might entail – complete self-forgetfulness, utter self-abandonment. As John describes it:

Day and night they never stop saying:

> *'Holy, holy, holy,*
> *is the Lord God Almighty,*
> *who was, and is, and is to come . . .'*

Then I looked and heard the voice of many angels, numbering thousands upon thousands, and ten thousand times ten thousand. They encircled the throne and the living creatures and the elders. In a loud voice they sang:

> *'Worthy is the Lamb, who was slain, to receive power*
> *and wealth and wisdom and strength*
> *and honour and glory and praise!'*

Then I heard every creature in heaven and on earth and under the earth and on the sea, and all that is in them, singing:

> *'To him who sits on the throne and to the Lamb*
> *be praise and honour and glory and power,*
> *for ever and ever!'*

The four living creatures said, 'Amen,' and the elders fell down and worshipped.

(Revelation 4:8; 5:11–14)

I am tempted to say, 'Fantastic!' and to leave it at that. But there is more. Zephaniah puts it beautifully:

> *Do not fear . . . do not let your hands hang limp. The Lord your God is with you, he is mighty to save. He will take great delight in you, he will quiet you with his love, he will rejoice over you with singing. (3:16–17)*

There is a sense in which that prophecy has already been fulfilled. There is another sense in which we have yet to enter into a full experiential awareness of its meaning. Here in this world, God's felt presence is, at best, fleeting, intermittent, transitory. Not so in heaven: there we shall enjoy a permanent intimacy with God. There, we shall know, not with the eye of faith, but experientially that we belong to God and that he belongs to us. There the words from the Song of Solomon will find their fulfilment: 'I am my Beloved's, and my Beloved is mine' (6:3 JB).

We shall know what it means to be the Bride of Christ. Michael Wilcock's description of the heavenly Bride never ceases to excite me:

> *We have passed beyond the bounds of space and time into regions of eternal light, unshadowed by the slightest imperfection, not to say evil; where the eyes of every created thing are fixed in adoration upon the Lamb alone.* Yet he is not alone. *For sharing the Scene with him – indeed, taking its very title role – is a radiant stranger whose features, as we consider them, are nonetheless familiar. Can it be . . .?*
>
> *It is 'the Bride, the wife of the Lamb.' It is the church of Christ.* It is you; it is I. *Whatever other metaphors we may use to describe our relationship with Christ, the last Scene of the Bible shows us ourselves married to him, 'cleansed . . . by the washing of water with the word', presented before him 'in splendour, without spot or wrinkle or any such thing.' (Ephesians 5:26–7)*
>
> *Even so, come Lord Jesus!*[2,3]

Reflection

What words would you use to describe your emotions as you anticipate being encountered by Christ eternally?

What gives rise to these emotions? Tell God your findings in a written or a verbal prayer:

If you feel you can, pray this prayer: 'Yes! Come, Master Jesus!'

Finally, take time to look back over anything you have written or drawn during the past month – or however long it has taken you to work through this book. Ask yourself the following questions:

How has God come to me while I have been using this book?

What, in particular, has he said to me which I need to heed for now?

What resolves, if any, have I made? Or, in the light of what I have discovered, what resolutions would it be helpful for me to make?

Notes

Unless otherwise stated, the publishers are Hodder & Stoughton

Introduction
1. Carlo Carretto, *The God Who Comes*, Darton, Longman and Todd 1974, p.3.
2. Ibid, pp.xv–xvi.

Chapter 1
1. Joyce Huggett, *Prayer Journal*, Marshall Pickering 1988.

Chapter 2
1. Eugene Peterson's paraphrase of the New Testament, *The Message*, Nav. Press 1993, p.520.
2. Joyce Huggett, *Listening to Others*, 1988, pp.55–6.
3. Eugene Peterson's paraphrase.
4. Eugene Peterson's paraphrase of Revelation 2:5.
5. Quoted in Joyce Huggett, *Open to God*, 1986, p.18.

Chapter 3
1. Joyce Huggett, *Listening to God*, pp.32–4.
2. Maria Boulding, *The Coming of God*, SPCK 1982, quoted in Joyce Huggett, *Open to God*.

Chapter 4

1. Joyce Huggett, *Finding God in the Fast Lane*, Eagle 1993, pp.56, 59, 60.
2. Jackie Pullinger, *Crack in the Wall*, 1988, quoted in Joyce Huggett, op.cit., p.60.

Chapter 5

1. Joyce Huggett, *The Smile of Love*, 1990, pp.36–7.
2. Joyce Huggett, *Holy Days and Holidays*, BRF, Fifth Day.

Chapter 6

1. Guy Brinkworth SJ, *Thirsting for God*, Mullan Press 1970, pp.7–8.
2. George Sinker, *Jesus Loved Martha*, St Hughe's Press 1949, p.11.
3. Ibid, p.12.
4. Ibid, p.14.
5. Joyce Huggett, *Open to God*, pp.27–9.
6. David Adam, *Tides and Seasons*, SPCK Triangle 1989, p.20, quoted in Joyce Huggett, *Finding God in the Fast Lane*, by permission of the publishers.
7. Eric Milner-White, *My God, My Glory*, SPCK Triangle 1994, p.17 (slightly adapted). Used by permission of the publishers.

Chapter 7

1. Joyce Huggett, *Listening to God*, pp.101–3.

Chapter 8

1. Joyce Huggett, *Finding Freedom*, 1994, p.61.
2. Joyce Huggett, *Listening to God*, 1986, pp.210–11.

3. Jim Packer, *God's Words*, IVP 1981, p.35, quoted in Joyce Huggett, *Listening to God*, p.211.

Chapter 9
1. Joyce Huggett, *The Smile of Love*, p.79–84.

Chapter 10
1. Joyce Huggett, *Finding Freedom*, pp.79–81.

Chapter 11
1. Joyce Huggett, *Listening to Others*, pp.256–7.

Chapter 12
1. Kevin O'Shea CSSR, *The Way of Tenderness*, Paulist Press 1978, pp.9–10.
2. Joyce Huggett, *Finding Freedom*, pp.110–12.

Chapter 13
1. Joyce Huggett, *Listening to Others*, pp.141–3.

Chapter 14
1. Quoted in Joyce Huggett, *Listening to Others*, source unknown.
2. Joyce Huggett, *Just Good Friends*, IVP 1993, pp.127–8.

Chapter 15
1. Vera Phillips and Edwin Robertson, *The Wounded Healer*, SPCK Triangle 1984, p.103.

2. Joyce Huggett, *Listening to Others*, pp.211–12.

Chapter 16
1. Jean Vanier, *Treasures of the Heart: Daily Readings with Jean Vanier*, DLT 1989, p.14.
2. Adapted from Joyce Huggett, *Under the Caring Eye of God*, Eagle 1991, pp.175–7.

Chapter 17
1. Joyce Huggett, *Finding Freedom*, pp.9, 10.

Chapter 18
1. Joyce Huggett, *Creative Conflict*, IVP (USA) 1984, pp.11–12.
2. Ibid, pp.19–20.

Chapter 19
1. Joyce Huggett, *Marriage Matters*, Eagle 1987, pp.122–4.

Chapter 20
1. Joyce Huggett, *Finding God in the Fast Lane*, Eagle 1993, pp.60–4.

Chapter 22
1. Joyce Huggett, *The Smile of Love*, p.14.

Chapter 23
1. Sheila Cassidy, *Sharing the Darkness*, DLT 1988.
2. Joyce Huggett, *Under the Caring Eye of God*, pp.119–22, 48.

Chapter 24
1. Joyce Huggett, *The Smile of Love*, pp.187–9.

Chapter 25
1. Jean Vanier, *The Broken Body*, Darton, Longman and Todd 1988, p.118.
2. Joyce Huggett, *Finding Freedom*, pp.146–8.

Chapter 26
1. Paul Gurr, *'Come as you are'*, Richmond, Australia: Spectrum Publications Pty Ltd. This song can be heard on the cassette *God's Springtime*, Joyce Huggett, Eagle.
2. Joyce Huggett, *Under the Caring Eye of God*, Eagle 1991, pp.127–30.

Chapter 27
1. Joyce Huggett, *Finding Freedom*, pp.32, 37, 38.

Chapter 28
1. William Barclay, *The Gospel of Matthew*, Vol. 2, Saint Andrew Press 1975, p.60.
2. Joyce Huggett, *Listening to God*, pp.167–70.

Chapter 29
1. Joyce Huggett, *Finding Freedom*, pp.140–2.
2. *The Spiritual Exercises of St Ignatius of Loyola*, ed. Halcyon Backhouse, Hodder and Stoughton, 1989.

Chapter 30

1. C.S. Lewis, *The Last Battle*, Puffin 1964, p.165.
2. Michael Wilcock, *I Saw Heaven Opened*, IVP 1975, p.205.
3. Joyce Huggett, *Finding Freedom*, pp.174–7.